DATE DUE

The Imagery Debate

Representation and Mind
Hilary Putnam and Ned Block, editors

The Imagery Debate

Michael Tye

A Bradford Book
The MIT Press
Cambridge, Massachusetts
London, England

This book was set in Palatino by DEKR Corporation and was printed and bound in the United States of America.

Library of Congress Cataloging-in-Publication Data

Tye, Michael.
  The imagery debate / Michael Tye.
      p.   cm.—(Representation and mind)
  "A Bradford book."
  Includes bibliographical references and index.
  ISBN 0-262-20086-4
  1. Imagery (Psychology) 2. Mental representation. I. Title.
II. Series.
BF367.T94   1991
153.3'2.—dc20   91-7423
                                                                              CIP

For Lauretta

Contents

Acknowledgments

Parts of the book have been read at colloquia and conferences in both philosophy and cognitive science at Harvard University, King's College Cambridge, King's College London, SUNY at Buffalo, Temple University, and the University of California at Santa Barbara. I am grateful to Justin Broakes, David Delameter, Catherine Hanson, Terry Horgan, Brian McLaughlin, Christopher Peacocke, Lauretta Reeves, Sydney Shoemaker, Michael Thau, and William Tolhurst for helpful comments. I am especially indebted to Ned Block, both for initially getting me interested in research on imagery in psychology and for providing me with a number of very useful criticisms. Portions of chapter 3 are drawn from my article "The Picture Theory of Mental Images," *The Philosophical Review* 97 (1988), pp. 497–520. I would like to thank the editors and publishers for permission to make use of this work.

Introduction

There has been a remarkable revival of interest in mental imagery among psychologists after a long period of neglect. It is now considered respectable again to talk of people having mental images and to inquire into their role in cognition. A large body of experimental data has been gathered and theories have been proposed. By and large, the theories fall into two groups: those that liken mental images to pictures and those that liken them to linguistic descriptions. Advocates of the pictorial view grant that we do not literally have pictures in our heads when we image things. But they insist nevertheless that the experimental data are best explained by the hypothesis that our images represent in something like the manner of pictures. Advocates of the descriptional approach argue that the experimental evidence cited by pictorialists can be accommodated without supposing that any of our inner representations have a picture-like structure. In their view, it suffices to maintain that images represent in the manner of many nonimagistic mental representations, namely, in the manner of language. The controversy that has raged between the two groups has come to be called the "imagery debate."

This book is, in part, about the imagery debate so understood. But it also has a wider focus; for imagery has been extensively discussed in philosophy, both historically and in the twentieth century. Some of the questions philosophers have debated remain largely untouched by the current debate in psychology, whereas others are at the forefront of the present controversy. My overall aim is to show how the philosophical and psychological theories relate to one another and to propose a comprehensive view of imagery, one that not only tackles the issue of imagistic representation but also provides answers to questions concerning the subjective, phenomenal aspects of imagery, image indeterminacy, the physical basis of imagery, and the causal role of image content.

The title of the book, then, refers to the imagery debate in both philosophy and psychology—the imagery debates, if you will, that have taken place in both arenas. What I have attempted to do is both to comment upon and to enter into (or, in one instance, dissolve) these various debates. In the case of the debate in psychology about imagistic representation, for example, I argue that both pictorialist and descriptionalist theories encounter difficulties of one sort or another, and I make a "mixed" proposal of my own that is influenced most strongly by the views of Stephen Kosslyn and David Marr. In a sense, then, I am wearing two hats. Donning my customary headgear, I am working as a philosopher trying to clarify conceptual issues. Switching into my other hat, I am playing the part of a cognitive scientist with an account of imagistic representation that is to be tested against the experimental evidence.

I was led to attempt this mixed project for several reasons. First, the imagery debate in psychology is not an easy controversy to understand. Coming to grips with it requires unraveling a web of empirical and conceptual issues. As I read the literature, I came to think that these issues had not been properly clarified by the participants in the debate and that there were serious misunderstandings of the various viewpoints. Second, given the plentiful evidence that there are shared mechanisms in imagery and vision, it seemed to me that it would be worthwhile to look at the imagery debate in psychology from the perspective of Marr's seminal work on vision. This, then, led me to the proposal mentioned above. Finally, I was struck by the fact that there was no up-to-date comprehensive theory of mental imagery, no theory, that is, that unites and illuminates both philosophical and psychological perspectives.

I have written the book in a manner that is, I hope, generally accessible. No prior acquaintance with the imagery debate in psychology is necessary in order to follow my survey or my own contribution to the debate, and no real background in philosophy is presupposed by my presentation of the philosophical views. The various chapters may be summarized as follows:

In chapter 1, I review important positions in the history of philosophy, beginning with Aristotle and continuing through Descartes, the British Empiricists, and Kant. The two most popular positions historically were the view that images are picture-like representations and the view that imagining is like perceiving in less than optimal conditions (so that imagining a giraffe, say, is like seeing a giraffe through a mist or a sheet of gauze). Philosophers typically defended these views by appeal to introspection: allegedly, one's awareness of one's own mental life makes it obvious that both views are correct.

I argue that the appeal to introspection is badly flawed. The conclusion I draw is that historical accounts of the nature of mental images and their role in cognition are without a secure foundation.

Chapter 2 addresses the decline of the picture theory of images in recent philosophy and the emergence of alternative positions. This century, philosophers have come to realize that the pictorial approach to imagery is really very puzzling. After all, images are not viewed with real eyes; they cannot be hung on real walls; they have no objective weight or color. So what can it mean to say that mental images are like pictures? Many philosophers recently have despaired of making sense of the pictorial approach and have opted for alternative views. I lay out the contemporary philosophical objections to the picture theory, and I explain the three major alternative positions.

In chapter 3, I discuss the reemergence of the picture theory in cognitive psychology. The leading advocate of the picture theory in this context is Stephen Kosslyn. If Kosslyn is correct that the pictorial view provides the best explanation for a wide variety of experimental results, then it appears that the historical philosophers had the right conception of imagery after all (though for the wrong reasons). Kosslyn's position, however, is not straightforward, and it has generated considerable confusion in the writings of critics and supporters alike. My primary aim in this chapter is to present a clear statement of Kosslyn's view and the experimental data that it is supposed to illuminate. I also bring out one alternative way, closely related to Kosslyn's, in which the picture theory may be elucidated.

Chapter 4 is concerned with the view that mental images are structural descriptions. There are a number of important cognitive scientists who maintain that Kosslyn's approach is misguided and that images are better viewed on the model of inner descriptions (so that an image of a frog, say, is really more like a description of a frog's shape than a picture of a frog). I explain the two best-known versions of this linguistic conception of imagery, and I relate them to one of the alternative philosophical accounts sketched in chapter 2. I also elaborate the experimental evidence that proponents of the linguistic view adduce in defense of their position.

In chapter 5, I present my own view of the manner in which images represent objects in the world. The line I take is essentially a hybrid one: I maintain that images are interpreted symbol-filled arrays, where such arrays are in certain respects like pictures and in others like linguistic representations. Since my position incorporates insights not only from Kosslyn's work on imagery but also from Marr's account of vision, I briefly summarize the key components of Marr's theory. I also comment on the issue of visual and spatial representation in imagery, and I elaborate a number of objections of my own to the pictorial and descriptive approaches.

Chapter 6 is an account of the nature and origins of the vagueness that infects many mental images with reference to the claims made by both philosophers and psychologists. This account also incorporates a discussion of various relevant aspects of the process of image generation from information in long-term memory.

In chapter 7, I explore the phenomenal aspects of mental imagery. It is very widely held in philosophy that mental images have, over and above their representational contents, intrinsic, introspectively accessible qualities in virtue of which they have those contents. On this view, a mental image of a zebra, for example, has certain intrinsic qualities accessible to consciousness in virtue of which it represents a zebra. This is supposedly why imaging a zebra "feels" different from merely thinking of a zebra without forming any image: in the latter case, one's mental representation lacks the phenomenal qualities or visual qualia, as they are sometimes called, that are present in the former. I maintain that this whole conception of the phenomenal or subjective character of mental images is mistaken, and I defend an alternative account.

In chapter 8, I discuss the physical basis of imagery and the causal role of image content: how imagery is realized in the brain, and how the contents of images can be causally relevant to behavior. I consider the first question both with respect to the neuropsychological data on image generation and with respect to two versions of philosophical materialism concerning mental images. To illustrate the subject matter of the second question, suppose you form an image of a snake and suppose you have a snake phobia. Your image may cause you to perspire. In the event that this happens, it is the fact that your image has the content it does (the fact that it is an image of a *snake* and not of a bird, say) that is responsible for its causing you to perspire. If, as seems likely, a complete neurophysiological account may be given of the origins of your perspiring, how is it possible for the content of your image (apparently not a neurophysiological property) to make any difference to your behavior? And what reason is there to suppose that the content of your image is causally efficacious in this instance, given that the contents of things elsewhere are sometimes causally inert, as, for example, when the pitch, but not the content, of the sounds produced by a soprano causes a glass to shatter?

The Imagery Debate

Chapter 1

Imagery in the History of Philosophy

Imagery has played an enormously important role in philosophical conceptions of the mind. But philosophers have not always agreed on just how broad this role is; nor have they always agreed on the nature of imagery itself. The two most popular views in philosophy prior to this century have been what we might call the "picture theory" and the "weak percept theory." According to the former view, mental images—specifically, visual images—are significantly picture-like in the way they represent objects in the world. According to the latter view, imagining is like perceiving in less than optimal conditions. Amplified a little, the basic claim of the weak percept theory is that the impressions made in memory from data supplied by the senses weaken with time of storage so that mental images generated from these stored impressions are generally less sharp than the corresponding percepts. Although both positions were widely accepted prior to this century, some philosophers had serious reservations about the lack of determinacy alleged to be present in mental images by advocates of the weak percept theory. There was also some debate about just how mental images pictorially represent external objects.

In section 1.1, I summarize the major traditional philosophical accounts of imagery, and I discuss the most significant disagreements that arose among advocates of these accounts. This is intended not only to illuminate the early philosophical perspectives but also to provide an historical background against which contemporary views on imagery may be located. In section 1.2, I examine the evidence upon which the traditional accounts rest.

Before we proceed, a quick comment is in order on my usage of the terms "image" and "imagine." Starting with chapter 3, the term "image" is applied exclusively to *visual* images. In chapters 1 and 2, the context should make it clear whether the term is restricted to the visual case or not. The same holds true for the term "imagine."

1.1 Traditional Philosophical Accounts of Imagery

Aristotle appears to have held that mental images are like inner pictures. Consider, for example, these passages:

> . . . we can call up a picture, as in the practice of mnemonics, by the use of mental images . . .[1]

> The nature of memory and its process has now been explained as the persistent possession of an image, in the sense of a copy of the thing to which the image refers, and it has been further explained to what faculty in us this belongs, viz. to the primary power of sensation . . .[2]

The account of representational content Aristotle endorses here is one that proved very popular with later philosophers. Mental images, according to Aristotle, must resemble or copy what they represent. The thought lying behind this claim is presumably that real pictures must resemble what is pictured and not just represent it by playing a conventional symbolic role. Thus, if mental images are inner pictures, they must represent in like fashion.

Aristotle seems to have come to the view that mental images are picture-like via the evidence afforded by introspection. When we introspect, we find that having a mental image is like looking at a picture. So, of course, mental images are themselves like pictures. This introspective defense of the picture theory is one that Aristotle shared with all subsequent philosophers who accepted the picture theory prior to the advent of recent work in cognitive psychology on imagery. Later in this chapter, we shall consider at some length the merits of such a defense. For the moment, I merely wish to comment on a passage in *On the Soul* in which Aristotle makes a related claim:

> . . . when we think something to be fearful or threatening, emotion is immediately produced, and so too with what is encouraging; but when we merely imagine we remain as unaffected as persons who are looking at a painting of some dreadful or encouraging scene.[3]

In this passage, Aristotle draws the parallel mentioned above between imagining and viewing a picture. Moreover, he claims that imagining never directly produces fear or any other emotion. Now why does Aristotle make this claim? It is tempting to suggest that he is again relying on introspection. Having introspected his own mental images, Aristotle draws a general conclusion about imagination and emotion. This conclusion is false, however, as is shown by recent therapeutic work that uses imagery to help people overcome phobias. It has been found that phobic people frequently become upset when they form mental images of the feared objects or situations. Indeed, they become almost as agitated as they would were the feared objects physically present. The degree of fear they experience varies with the ways the objects are imaged. For example, if you have a dog phobia, you'll be much more agitated if you image a full-grown Doberman near your hands than if you image a small poodle puppy curled up asleep inside a cage. Thus, the procedure adopted in therapy is to get patients initially to form images they feel relatively comfortable with and later to form more and more threatening images without their becoming tense or fearful. Once the patients show no anxiety with images of the feared objects, they can typically face the real objects without fear too.

The sort of introspectively based armchair theorizing that seems to underlie Aristotle's view of imagination and its separation from emotion is commonplace in the history of philosophy. And just as it leads Aristotle astray here, so too it leads others astray elsewhere, as we shall shortly see.

There are passages in Aristotle's work that, under some translations, suggest that Aristotle holds that mental images are crucial to all thought.[4] Such a view seems incompatible with the position just cited in which Aristotle draws a sharp distinction between thinking something to be fearful and imagining the same. There is also independent reason to doubt that the relevant translations accurately capture Aristotle's intent.[5] Whatever Aristotle's real position here, another philosopher, who certainly does maintain that imagining something is quite unlike thinking or conceiving of it, is Rene Descartes. This comes out very clearly in his discussion of the case of the chiliagon in *Meditation Six*.[6]

According to Descartes, we can easily imagine a pentagon in a way that is introspectively distinguishable from our imagining a hexagon. But, Descartes tells us, we *cannot* imagine a chiliagon (a 1000-sided figure) in a way that is distinct from imagining a 999-sided figure. By contrast, we have no difficulty at all in *conceiving* of a chiliagon and how it differs from a figure with one more or less sides. The conclusion Descartes explicitly draws is that imagining is not the same as (nor a component of) thinking or conceiving. A further conclusion is indicated, however. For one plausible explanation of our inability to imagine a 1000-sided figure in a way that is experientially distinguishable from our imagining a 999-sided figure is that imagining is like seeing in a glance. Thus, just as seeing a chiliagon is experientially no different from seeing a figure with one fewer side, so imagining the former figure is no different from imagining the latter. This view, that imaging is like seeing, is one that Descartes seems to have held even though it does not surface in connection with his discussion of the chiliagon. For example, in *Meditation Three*, Descartes states that only those thoughts that "are, so to speak, pictures" are properly called "ideas" and also that some ideas "proceed from certain things outside us."[7] The latter ideas are percepts. Thus, Descartes takes mental images to include percepts as well as images conjured up by the will. This seems intelligible only on the assumption that imagining and perceiving are, at root, the same.

There are further a priori reasons for drawing a conceptual link between imagining and seeing. Just as I may be said to see an object even though not every part of the object is directly in my field of vision, so too I may be classified as imagining an object in parallel circumstances. Similarly, just as seeing is from a point of view, so too is imagining. For example, I cannot see the inside and outside of a room at the same time, unless I use mirrors, and neither can I imagine the inside and outside of a room at the same time, unless I imagine myself using mirrors.

Descartes's adherence to Aristotle's view that mental images copy the objects they represent comes out in the following passage from *Meditation Three*:

> My principal task in this place is to consider, in respect to those ideas which appear to me to proceed from certain objects that are outside me, what are the reasons which cause me to think them similar to these objects.[8]

Descartes here is wondering what justification he has for believing that percepts are similar to the objects they represent. Later in the *Meditations*, having proven the existence of God, Descartes finds the justification he desires. This justification need not concern us in the present context. The salient point for our purposes is that Descartes, like Aristotle, holds that percepts (and mental images) copy objects in the external world.

Thomas Hobbes's discussion of imagery is noteworthy in three respects. First, Hobbes emphasizes the vagueness or lack of determinacy in many mental images as well as the parallel with seeing. For example:

> . . . after the object is removed or the eye shut, we still retain an image of the thing seen, though more obscure than when we see it.[9]

And any object being removed from our eyes, though the impression it made in us remain, yet other objects more present succeeding and working on us, the imagination of the past is obscured and made weak, as the voice of a man is in the noise of the day. From whence it follows that the longer the time is after the sight or sense of any object, the weaker is the imagination.[10]

Second, Hobbes presents the beginnings of an account of the generation of mental images. On Hobbes's view, mental images are not like slides or photographs that are stored in memory and taken out whenever the experience of imagery occurs. As Hobbes is aware, this model cannot explain our ability to form images of entirely novel scenes (as, for example, when a frog is imaged leaping over a rhinoceros). Rather, in Hobbes's view, images may be generated by combining separate percepts stored in memory. He says:

Again, imagination being only of those things which have been formerly perceived by sense, either all at once or by parts at several times, the former, which is the imagining the whole object as it was presented to the sense, is simple imagination, as when one imagines a man or horse which he has seen before. The other is compounded, as when, from the sight of a man at one time and of a horse at another, we conceive in our mind a centaur.[11]

Third, in sharp contrast with Descartes, Hobbes locates imagery within the brain.[12]

With Locke, Berkeley, and Hume, imagery takes center stage in the mind, or rather, it occupies the entire stage; for, unlike Descartes and Hobbes, the British Empiricists held that *all* thought consists in the manipulation of either simple images derived from sense experience or complex images built up from these simple images. If we consider first John Locke, we find, for example, that memory is taken to consist in the retention of images, that the classification or identification of objects is taken to consist in the checking or comparison of objects and images, and that learning a language is taken to consist in associating sounds and images.[13] Images, in turn, for Locke are mental pictures. He says, speaking of images (or "ideas," to use his preferred term):

. . . there is an ability in the mind when it will revive them again, and as it were paint them anew on itself, though some with more, some with less difficulty . . . .[14]

A little later, he comments:

> The ideas of the nurse and mother are well framed in their minds (i.e., the minds of children); and, like pictures of them, represent only those individuals.[15]

Interestingly, in the following passage, Locke seems to repudiate the pictorial approach to imagery:

> To discover the nature of our ideas the better, and to discourse of them intelligibly, it will be convenient to distinguish them as they are ideas or perceptions in our minds, and as they are modifications of matter in the bodies that cause such perception in us: that so we may not think (as perhaps usually is done) that they are exactly the images and resemblances of something inherent in the subject; most of those of sensation being in the mind no more the likeness of something existing without us, than the names that stand for them are the likeness of our ideas, which yet upon hearing they are apt to excite in us.[16]

It is hard to reconcile Locke's position here with what he says elsewhere (including the two other passages above). Perhaps Locke's underlying intention is to reject the thesis that ideas get their representational content via resemblance while nonetheless holding on to the thesis that ideas are like pictures. If this is what Locke has in mind, then he obviously needs to say much more about just what makes ideas picture-like.

In any event, according to Locke, the ideas or images stored in memory are abstract, as are the ideas used in classification and the ideas that function as word meanings. This claim, that ideas are sometimes abstract, is at bottom the claim that ideas are sometimes sketchy or lacking in detail. Locke's position seems to be that the senses provide us with ideas or percepts that are fully determinate. These ideas are then stripped of some of their internal details as well as the particular circumstances associated with their arrival in the mind. Thus, Locke says:

> [T]he mind makes the particular ideas received from particular objects to become general; which is done by considering them as they are in the mind such appearances,—separate from all other existences, and the circumstances of real existence, as time, place, or any other concomitant ideas. This is called ABSTRACTION, whereby ideas taken from particular beings become general representatives of all of the same kind;[17]

It appears, then, that on Locke's view, certain ideas are developed by abstraction from particular ideas received from particular objects. The former ideas are copies of the latter, but the process of copying is such that various details are left out. On this understanding of Locke, his doctrine of abstract ideas is part and parcel of his version of what I earlier called the "weak percept theory."

It seems evident that Locke (and his fellow Empiricists) gave imagery too broad a role in the theater of the mind. For one thing, Locke's assimilation of the sensory to the intellectual ignores the lesson that should have been learned from Descartes's discussion of the chiliagon. For another, there are many, many words whose meanings we understand even though we cannot conjure up an appropriate image. Consider, for example, "sake," "conduct," "electron." Moreover, even though images *sometimes* guide us in linguistic contexts, as Wittgenstein observed,[18] they cannot always do so. Suppose, for example, that you tell me to form a mental image of a tulip. If acting on a linguistic command requires first framing the appropriate image, then in order to obey you, *prior* to doing so, I must form a mental image of a tulip. However, that is impossible. As soon as I form the image, I have already obeyed you.

There are passages in George Berkeley's writings that seem to suggest that he appreciated these points about meaning and language. He asserts, for example, that words can be meaningful even when not associated with ideas. However, it is not clear that Berkeley was really opposed to the heart of the Lockean view. For Berkeley can be read as accepting the thesis that if a word is understood by a given person, P, then P must be capable of producing the relevant idea, even if, upon occasion, P uses the word without *actually* associating it with that idea. This interpretation of Berkeley's view fits nicely with the following passage:

> . . . a little attention will discover that it is not necessary (even in the strictest reasonings) that significant names which stand for ideas should, every time they are used, excite in the understanding the ideas they are made to stand for.[19]

There can be no doubt, however, that Berkeley disagrees strongly with Locke on the topic of abstract ideas. Berkeley accepts that mental images and percepts are items of the same type (ideas) and that mental images are frequently generated by combining percepts stored in memory. But Berkeley insists that every idea must have a definite shape and color, that vagueness or indeterminacy has no place in ideas themselves. Just why Berkeley holds this doctrine is not altogether clear. One possible explanation is that Berkeley is wedded to the received view that mental images are inner pictures. Unlike Locke, however, Berkeley thinks of pictures as we would think of clear photographs. Berkeley holds this photographic view of mental pictures, in turn, because it is dictated, he thinks, by introspection. He says:

> [F]or myself, I find indeed I have a faculty of imagining, or representing to myself, the ideas of those particular things I have perceived, and of variously compounding and dividing them. I can imagine a man with two heads, or the upper parts of a man joined to the body of a horse. I can consider the hand, the eye, the nose, each by itself abstracted or separated from the rest of the body. But then whatever hand or eye I imagine, it must have some particular shape and color. Likewise the idea of a man that I frame to myself must be either of a white, or a black, or a tawny, a straight, or a crooked, a tall, or a low, or a middle-sized man.[20]

If Berkeley is indeed denying the existence of *any* less than fully determinate images, then his position seems problematic. For it is surely not difficult to imagine a striped tiger, say, without thereby imagining a definite number of stripes. Likewise, to take the case Berkeley considers above, can one not imagine a man without specifying imaginatively the man's color or size? If one's images are anything like drawn sketches, the answer is obviously yes.

Now Berkeley believes not merely that Locke's doctrine of abstract ideas is inconsistent with the act of introspection but also that Lockean abstract ideas are logically impossible. Consider, for example, the following passage in which Berkeley first quotes Locke and then ridicules his view:

> To give the reader a yet clearer view of the nature of abstract ideas and the uses they are thought necessary to, I shall add one more passage out of the *Essay on Human Understanding*, which is as follows:
>
>> Abstract ideas are not so obvious or easy to children or the yet unexercised mind as particular ones. If they seem so to grown men it is only because by constant and familiar use they are made so. For when we nicely reflect upon them, we shall find that general ideas are fictions and contrivances of the mind, that carry difficulty with them, and do not so easily offer themselves as we are apt to imagine. For example, does it not require some pain and skill to form the general idea of a triangle (which is yet none of the most

abstract, comprehensive, and difficult); for it must be neither oblique nor rectangle, neither equilateral, equicrural, nor scalenon, but all and none of these at once? In effect, it is something imperfect that cannot exist, an idea wherein some parts of several different and inconsistent ideas are put together.

If any man has the faculty of framing in his mind such an idea of a triangle as is here described, it is in vain to pretend to dispute him out of it, nor would I go about it. All I desire is that the reader would fully and certainly inform himself whether he has such an idea or no. And this, methinks, can be no hard task for anyone to look a little into his own thoughts, and there try whether he has, or can attain to have, an idea that shall correspond with the description that is here given of the general idea of a triangle, which is "neither oblique nor rectangle, neither equilateral, equicrural nor scalenon, but all and none of these at once"?[21]

Although Berkeley certainly has a point here, his rejection of Lockean abstract ideas is, I think, too hasty. For Locke, in the passage Berkeley quotes, seems to have forgotten that his abstract ideas are formed by a copying process that *strips* percepts of various details and not by a process that *adds* any properties. Thus, when Locke says that the abstract idea of a triangle must be "neither oblique nor rectangle, neither equilateral, equicrural nor scalenon," in adding "*but all and none of these at once*," he overstates and confuses his case. What he should have said is simply "none of these at once." Such a statement would have been consistent with the core of the Lockean view, and Berkeley would no longer have been able to charge that Locke's abstract ideas are *logically* impossible.[22] Admittedly, Berkeley could still argue that ideas cannot be abstract to the degree that Locke supposes. But, to take one example, the case of stick figure drawings shows that pictures—and hence ideas, if ideas are like pictures—can be very sketchy indeed. So Berkeley's attack on Locke, as it stands, is very far from decisive.

The third British Empiricist, David Hume, has views on ideas that are obviously much influenced by Locke and Berkeley. According to Hume, thinking consists in the manipulation of ideas. Understanding a word is a matter of associating the right idea with it. And ideas are the "faint images" of sense impressions. Thus, Hume endorses the assimilation of the sensory to the intellectual, and he also accepts the weak percept theory. Moreover, he relies heavily on what he supposes is demonstrated by introspection. For example, he argues that the self is nothing but a bundle of different "perceptions" on the grounds that

> . . . when I enter most intimately into what I call *myself* I always stumble on some particular perception or other, of heat or cold, light or shade, love or hatred, pain or pleasure. I never can catch *myself* at any time without a perception, and never can observe anything but the perception.[23]

On the issue of Lockean abstract ideas, Hume sides with Berkeley. In Hume's view, Berkeley refuted Locke's theory of abstract ideas. Given that Hume was prepared to grant that some ideas are sketchy, this rejection of Locke's position is no doubt in part due to Berkeley's attack on the unfortunate passage from Locke's *Essay* quoted earlier. However, Hume is also motivated by a desire to give a plausible account of representational content for ideas. Let me explain.

Suppose I wish to teach you some geometrical point about triangles, though no one triangle in particular. On Locke's view, when I use the word "triangle," and you hear me, we both form the abstract idea of a triangle. There are, then, two tokens of the very same abstract idea. But what gives this idea its content? Evidently, it can't closely resemble any *particular* triangle. For if it did, it wouldn't be abstract. Perhaps, then, it gets its content via its *interpretation* by the person or persons having this idea. But if what gives an idea its content is at least in part its interpretation, then no *abstract* idea is necessary. So long as when I use the word "triangle" I form an idea that I interpret as representing triangles generally and you do likewise, we may understand one another perfectly well even if our ideas *in themselves* have little in common. Thus, Hume says:

> . . . the image in the mind is only that of a particular object, tho' the application of it in our reasoning be the same as if it were universal.[24]

It is important to realize that Hume is not here giving up the picture theory of mental images. Rather, Hume's insight is that resemblance is not sufficient for pictorial representation, that interpretation must play a crucial role. Kant, incidentally, seems to have shared Hume's insight in the following passage:

> Indeed it is schemata, not images of objects, which underlie our pure sensible concepts. No image could ever be adequate to the concept of a triangle in general. It would never attain that universality of the concept which renders it valid of all triangles, whether right-angled, obtuse-angled, or acute-angled; it would

always be limited to a part only of this sphere. The schema of the triangle can exist nowhere but in thought. It is a rule of synthesis of the imagination, in respect to pure figures in space.[25]

I might add that Hume's distinction between the claim that something is a picture of an *F* and the claim that something resembles an *F* is echoed in the writings of a number of philosophers this century. Nelson Goodman, for example, says:

> . . . unlike representation, resemblance is symmetric: B is as much like A as A is like B, but while a painting may represent the Duke of Wellington, the Duke doesn't represent the painting. Furthermore, in many cases neither one of a pair of very like objects represents the other: none of the automobiles off an assembly line is a picture of any of the rest; and a man is not normally a representation of another man, even his twin brother. Plainly, resemblance in any degree is no sufficient condition for representation.[26]

In a somewhat similar vein, Wittgenstein comments:

> I see a picture; it represents an old man walking up a steep path leaning on a stick. —How? Might it not have looked just the same if he had been sliding downhill in that position? Perhaps a Martian would describe the picture so. I do not need to explain why we do not describe it so.[27]

In summary, then, we may say that, by and large, philosophers historically held that mental images are picture-like representations similar to those occurring in perception. They frequently, but not always, allowed these representations to be sketchy or undetailed, and they frequently, but not always, took resemblance to be the picturing relation. They also sometimes exaggerated the role that imagery plays in mental activity generally. In opting for the basic pictorial view of images, they seem to have relied on the evidence allegedly afforded by introspection. And in delineating the boundaries of the realm of imagery, they relied on introspection together with armchair theorizing of one sort or another.

In section 1.2, I turn to a critical examination of these evidential bases for the historical views.

1.2 Critique of the Evidence upon which the Traditional Accounts Rest

Mental images *look* like the objects that they represent. In this respect, mental images are similar to realistic public pictures and dissimilar from other public representations, for example, descriptions. Hence, mental images represent in the manner of, or something very like the manner of, real pictures. This is the introspective argument for the pictorial approach to imagery in its simplest form. It has been enormously influential in shaping the views of philosophers historically. And it still has some appeal today. Unfortunately, the argument is badly flawed.

To begin with, the parallel between mental images and pictures is faulty. Although real public pictures do look like the objects that they represent, they do so only if they are *viewed* under the appropriate perceptual conditions (typically daylight at the distance from the picture intended by the artist for viewing) by perceivers whose perceptual apparatus is functioning normally. Mental images, however, are not *viewed* by imagers at all. Moreover, if mental images were viewed in daylight by normal perceivers via the use of cerebroscopes—and this, of course, would only be possible if mental images were neural entities, contrary to the claims of most historical philosophers—there is not the slightest reason to think that they would *then* look like the objects that they represent. After all, the fact that under one set of conditions an object O looks like another object O' obviously does not entail that under other quite different conditions O looks like O'. To take an extreme example, a dot on a blackboard looks like a ship viewed on the horizon but not like a ship a few hundred feet away.

Second, the reason that public pictures look like the objects that they represent when viewed under standard conditions is that in such conditions these pictures have the perceptible qualities they appear to have, and these perceptible qualities—in particular, certain spatial qualities—correspond to those of the represented objects. For example, if parts P_1, P_2, and P_3 in a picture represent object parts O_1, O_2, and O_3 respectively and O_1 is below O_2 and to O_3's left, as the object is seen from a certain point of view, then likewise P_1 is below P_2 and to P_3's left, as the picture is seen from a corresponding point of view. This correspondence of various spatial properties seems to be an important element in genuine pictorial representation. But, in the case of mental images, there is no *introspective* evidence that supports the claim that image parts *really* have *any* spatial properties, never mind ones that correspond to spatial properties of the represented objects. Moreover, if, as most historical philosophers supposed, mental images are nonphysical objects in the soul, then obviously mental images lack spatial properties. In this case, then, it *follows* that there is *no* spatial correspondence.

Finally, and more importantly, to assert that a mental image of my brother, say, looks to me like my brother is merely to assert that my imagistic experience is like the perceptual experience I undergo when I view my brother with my eyes. The latter assertion says nothing about *how* my brother is represented in my perceptual experience. He might be represented there pictorially, but equally he might be represented in some other way, for example, in some linguistic manner. Hence, the claim that mental images look like the object they represent *leaves open* the nature of this representation.[28]

To the objection that mental images don't look like words and hence cannot be representing in a linguistic manner, a similar response is appropriate. The claim that a mental image of my brother doesn't look to me like any public descriptions of my brother is simply the claim that the former imagistic experience isn't like the perceptual experiences I undergo when I train my eyes on various linguistic tokens representing my brother. Still, this is straightforwardly explicable on the hypothesis that my mental image represents my brother rather than certain words or descriptions for my brother. Thus, my mental image, like the representation involved in my perceptual experience, *could* be representing my brother linguistically.

Similarly, the fact that mental images are representations that look like pictures to their imagers does not support the picture theory. Imagistic experiences are like the perceptual experiences undergone when viewing the appropriate pictures. This is why mental images look like pictures. But whether the perceptual experiences *themselves* contain pictorial representations is an open question. And if this is open, so too is the same question for imagistic experiences.

I conclude that philosophers have been much too hasty in their almost universal acceptance prior to this century of the pictorial approach to imagery. If the picture theory rests solely on the testimony of introspection, then it is on very shaky ground indeed.

In the case of the weak percept theory of mental images, it seems to me that introspection is less misleading. Here introspection informs us that imagistic experiences are qualitatively like perceptual experiences although frequently fainter. Thus, introspection does support the claim that imagining is *phenomenally* rather like perceiving in less than optimal conditions.

The claim that introspection is reliable in this limited context fits well with the results of a famous psychological experiment conducted by C. W. Perky in 1910.[29] In this experiment, subjects in a room with normal lighting were asked to face a screen and to imagine a banana on it. Unknown to the subjects, a projector was set up behind the screen, containing a slide of a banana. Once the subjects reported that they had formed their images, the illumination on the projector was slowly increased so that it eventually cast a picture of a banana on the screen that was clearly visible to any newcomer entering the room. However, none of the subjects ever realized that they were looking at a real picture. Instead, they noticed merely that their "images" changed in certain ways—for example, their orientation—as time passed. This experiment seems to show that imaging is (at least sometimes) experientially indistinguishable from seeing. It thus adds independent weight to the view of the link between imaging and seeing that is presented by everyday introspection.

Turning finally to the role of imagery in mental activity generally, we again find a heavy reliance on introspection together with a priori armchair theorizing in the traditional philosophical accounts. It seems reasonable to hypothesize that one reason why historical philosophers often gave imagery such a prominent role in the mind is that they had no difficulty in *finding* images when they introspected. Of course, in some cases, images are all that they found (or so they said). Another related reason is that many philosophers subscribed to the view that the mind is wholly transparent to introspection. On this view, the claim that images are the sole mental objects accessible to introspection entails that there are no mental objects other than images.

It seems to me that we have excellent evidence for the falsity of the thesis that the mind is transparent to introspection. If this is indeed the case, if some of the workings of the mind are hidden from conscious view, then the question of the role that imagery plays in cognition generally is evidently not one that *could* be answered either by introspection directly or by armchair theorizing on the basis of introspection. Rather, it is a question for empirical investigation into the workings of the mind. In short, it is a question for cognitive psychology. I want now briefly to support my claim that the mind is not transparent to introspection. I also want to show how introspection can lead us badly astray when we try to use it in an attempt to discover how given introspectively accessible mental states are causally related.

In a well-known experiment conducted by James Lackner and Merrill Garrett, subjects were told to put on earphones and to listen *only* to the left channel.[30] In this channel, they heard the target sentence "The officer put out the lantern to signal the attack." In the other channel, half of the subjects were presented with sentences, the meanings of which clearly fixed the meaning of the target sentence and the ambiguous words "put out," and the other half were presented with altogether unrelated sentences (e.g., "The flowers have begun to bloom"). The members of both groups reported accurately the contents of the left channel, but no one could report the contents of the right channel. This was not merely because no one listened to the right channel. The sentences in that channel were played at a volume just low enough that no one could have reported accurately what the sentences were even if they *had* paid careful attention to the sounds coming from that channel.

The subjects were next given tests in which they had to decide on the meaning of the target sentence. Those who had been presented with unrelated sentences in the right channel were split over whether the target sentence meant that the officer placed the lantern outside or that the officer snuffed out the lantern. Those who had been presented with the related sentences (e.g., "The officer extinguished the lantern") overwhelmingly chose the same, correct interpretation.

The immediate conclusion warranted by this experiment is that the sentences in the unattended channel were understood by the subjects even though they were unable to report consciously on them. The point is not merely that these sentences were acoustically processed. Rather, their meanings were causally relevant to the interpretation the subjects chose, and hence the sentences were semantically processed. The general conclusion to which we are drawn is that at least some of our mental life is inaccessible to consciousness, in other words, that the mind is not wholly transparent to introspection. Of course, Lackner and Garrett's experiment does not tell us *how much* of our mental life is unconscious. Perhaps the amount accessible is but a tiny portion. If so, introspection will yield precious little information about our minds. In any event, the degree to which introspection reveals what is going on is to be determined not by a priori reflection but instead by empirical psychology.

Consider now an experiment conducted by Richard Nisbett and Timothy Wilson.[31] People in a shopping mall were asked to examine four identical nylon pantyhose and to rank them according to quality. It was found that the rightmost pantyhose were heavily preferred. On being asked whether position might have been a factor in their decisions, nearly all the people strongly denied it. In this experiment, introspection led people to the view that they formed the belief that the rightmost pantyhose were the best as a result of the visual and tactual sensations they experienced while viewing and handling those pantyhose. But introspection appears to have been badly wrong. Not only is there no reason to suppose that their sensations were any different in this one case than in the others but also what caused their belief was actually a factor they denied to be relevant, namely, the pantyhose position.

Here is another of Nisbett and Wilson's experiments where introspection misleads people about the causal links between mental states.[32] Two groups of subjects were shown filmed interviews with a college professor who had a Belgian accent. The interview seen by one group showed the professor speaking politely in a warm and pleasant manner. The interview seen by the other group showed the professor behaving in an intolerant and aloof manner. Subjects were asked to rate three physical features of the professor that were the same in both films—his mannerisms, accent, and physical appearance—and also to say how likable they found him overall. The first group of subjects liked both the professor and his physical features. The second group disliked the professor, and they found his physical features irritating. Given the invariance across films of the three physical features, these results indicate that the subjects' assessment of the professor's overall likability causally influenced their attitude toward the specific physical features. This causal influence was denied by both groups of subjects, however. Moreover, members of the second group wrongly believed (on the basis of introspection) that their negative attitude toward the professor's three physical features caused their negative assessment of his overall likability (rather than vice versa).

It appears, then, that introspection neither reveals all the mind's contents nor provides reliable information about the causal connections among those mental contents it does reveal.[33] The upshot is that questions about the role that a given kind of mental state (e.g., imagery) plays in the mind as a whole are best answered by empirical investigation into the mind and not by armchair theorizing based upon the fruits of introspection. This is, of course, widely acknowledged today. And, as we shall see later, cognitive psychologists have developed accounts of why we have mental images and the circumstances in which we do and do not use them. Historical philosophers took it upon themselves to develop their own accounts in isolation from any empirical work primarily because they thought that the mind and its workings were illuminated clearly and distinctly by the inner searchlight of introspection. This was a serious mistake, and it left historical accounts of the nature and role of mental imagery without a secure foundation. This is not to say that *none* of the historical arguments on imagery are sound. As I noted earlier, Descartes's thought experiment involving the chiliagon suggests a priori both that imaging is not experientially the same as understanding and that imaging is experientially like seeing. These, it seems to me, are significant points. But they are also very limited in their scope. For nothing is said either about just how imagery relates to understanding or about whether there are important similarities between imaging and seeing that are not revealed in experience. For insight into these matters, we must turn, I suggest, to contemporary cognitive psychology.

It is perhaps worth noting in conclusion that philosophers were not the only ones to place too heavy a reliance on introspection. In the 1890s, the early psychologists, notably William Wundt,[34] believed that the methodology of their field should be introspection. Moreover, they supposed that mental images are crucial to all thought. In holding these views, they were no doubt swayed by the writings of philosophers. And it was not until 1910–1913 under the influence of Oswaldo Kulpe and J. B. Watson that psychologists really began to free themselves from the introspective net. Kulpe's contribution was to discover empirically that some thoughts are not accompanied by mental images. The experiment he performed was very simple: Subjects lifted two objects of different weights (say, a book and a glass) one after another.[35] They were then asked to say which object was heavier. The subjects had no difficulty in answering, but they hadn't the faintest idea how they decided. They reported that they had no images at the time of their judgments. Kulpe concluded that there are things about the mind that introspection will not illuminate.

J. B. Watson's reaction was, of course, more extreme.[36] In Watson's view, earlier psychologists had been unscientific in paying *any* attention to subjective, introspective reports. Instead, psychologists should have studied only objective, verifiable stimuli and behavior. Thus began the movement in psychology known as behaviorism. I shall say something about behaviorism in the next chapter, the primary focus of which will be the major twentieth-century philosophical theories of imagery. As we shall see, some of these theories were themselves influenced by Watson's behaviorism.

Chapter 2

The Decline of the Picture Theory in Philosophy and the Emergence of Alternative Views

The picture theory of mental images has become much less popular in philosophy in recent years. In this chapter, I shall examine the major reasons for its diminishing support, and I shall investigate three important alternative approaches.

The chapter is divided into four sections. In section 2.1, I lay out the contemporary philosophical objections to the picture theory. In sections 2.2, 2.3, and 2.4, I introduce the three opposing theories, offering accounts of why these theories have emerged and what it is that they claim.

2.1 Philosophical Objections to the Picture Theory

Although the picture theory has lost the widespread support it once had in philosophy, it has not been without some notable advocates this century. G. E. Moore, Bertrand Russell, and H. H. Price, for example, all held that seeing the external world involves the apprehension of inner picture-like impressions, or "sense-data," as they are often called.[1] These sense-data are held to occur not only in veridical perception but also in hallucinations (as, for example, in the case of Macbeth when he said, "Is this a dagger which I see before me, / The handle toward my hand? Come let me clutch thee. / I have thee not, and yet I see thee still"). Moreover, sense-data can be conjured up by deliberate acts of the imagination, according to their advocates. Thus, the sense-data of the twentieth century are none other than the ideas and impressions of Locke, Berkeley, and Hume.

The sense-datum theory of visual perception and the parallel picture theory of mental imagery have come under severe attack, however, in the latter half of this century. Let us begin with some objections to the picture theory that are to be found in the work of Gilbert Ryle. In *The Concept of Mind*, Ryle argues that neither imagination nor seeing involves any inner mental pictures of which the subject is aware. In the case of imagination, Ryle claims that we think that there are mental pictures because the ordinary ways we speak naturally suggest such a view.[2] For example, we talk in everyday contexts of picturing objects when we imagine them. This naturally leads philosophers to suppose that there are mental entities corresponding to this talk. But the thesis that mental images are inner pictures is really very puzzling. Evidently, mental images are not viewed with real eyes. They cannot be placed in real frames. There is no genuine canvas or paint. Thus, philosophers have been led to the view that mental images are picture counterparts that are viewed with a mind's eye and that are located not in real space but instead in some ghostly realm. This is all a mistake, according to Ryle, fostered by the propensity of many philosophers to take ordinary language too literally. And it is certainly no less puzzling than the unhedged view that mental images are real pictures. For what is a mind's eye? Or a picture counterpart? And what is the connection between ghostly "space" and real space? Moreover, if, as adherents of the picture theory generally suppose, seeing the external world, like imaging, involves an inner "eye" seeing an inner "picture," then won't this latter seeing itself require a further inner "picture" and a further "eye" that sees it, and so on ad infinitum?

This objection evidently has substantial force. It seems to me, however, that Ryle is not obviously correct in his assertion that it is ordinary language that generates the picture view. For none of the historical philosophers actually cite linguistic usage as a reason for adopting the picture theory. Instead, they typically focus on the evidence afforded by introspection. Moreover, one possible account of why our ordinary talk of mental imagery seems to support the pictorial view is that introspection has led not only philosophers but also nonphilosophers to adopt that view and to enshrine it in our ordinary language. Still, it cannot be denied that the claim that mental images are inner pictures is very perplexing. And philosophers who made this claim said little to explain it. Admittedly, as we saw in chapter 1, most advocates of the picture theory held that mental images copy or resemble what they represent. But this is really not very helpful, for everything resembles everything in some respect or other. Nor does it improve matters to say that mental images closely resemble the objects that they represent, for it is far from clear what could ground such a close resemblance.

Another of Ryle's objections to the picture theory of mental images is also offered as an objection to the weak percept theory. This objection has been less influential than the one above, and it seems to me much less powerful. Ryle argues that mental images are not just played-back copies of original sensations, that mental images derive their representational content (at least in part) from how they are interpreted by their subjects. According to Ryle, if I vividly "see" something in my mind's eye, I must be able to identify what I "see." By contrast, if I peer at an object in the distance using my real eyes, I may not be able to say just what I see. This shows, Ryle claims, that imaging isn't like seeing and also that imaging isn't like observing a picture.[3] For just as one might be unable to identify an object in the distance, so too one might be unable to identify what a given real picture pictures (e.g., whether it portrays Tom Smith or his identical twin, Tim).

Ryle's initial point—that interpretation plays an essential role in determining imagistic content—is one that at least some of the historical picture theorists granted. Hume, for example, seems to have appreciated this point. Ryle's second claim, however, is contentious. Contra Ryle, surely it is possible to "see" something in one's mind's eye and yet fail to identify it. Suppose, for example, that I show you an object but you are unable to tell exactly what it is that you are seeing. Still, you can form a mental image *of* that very object. In this respect, having a mental image of one particular, real object is just like seeing that object. And, in this respect, a mental image itself need not come stamped with the correct identification of the kind of object imaged even if it is always associated with *some* interpretation, for example, as being an image of the object so-and-so is holding.

Here is another example. Suppose I get you to view an ambiguous figure and then form a mental image of it. Initially when you inspect your image, you may not be able to identify at all what the figure pictures. A little later, you may suddenly realize that your image is an image of a figure representing a duck. Perhaps later still, you "see" the alternative: your image is also an image of a figure representing a rabbit. Where Ryle goes wrong, I suggest, is in ignoring the distinction between having a mental image of one specific object (in which case, there must really be an object in the world which one is imaging) and having a mental image of an object of kind *F* (though no one object of kind *F* in particular). In the latter case, it seems plausible to hold that one must identify what is imaged as being an *F*. In the former case, however, there need be no such identification. What is true here for imaging is true also for seeing, it seems to me. The analogy to the latter case is seeing *that* there is an *F*; the analogy to the former is seeing an *F*.

A third objection of Ryle's[4] is that the familiar comparison of seen things and their likenesses (e.g., trees and their reflections or their photographs) makes it easy and tempting to describe visual imaging as if it involved looking at a likeness instead of the original. But such

an approach, Ryle claims, is entirely implausible for images associated with smell and taste. Suppose, to take Ryle's example, I vividly
"see" in my mind's eye the blacksmith's forge I used to visit in my
youth and I "smell" a singed hoof. Ordinary English doesn't permit
me to say, "I smell a copy of a singed hoof." Indeed, the very idea
of a distinction between smell and a copy of a smell is nonsensical.
Hence, just as we should reject the "copy" or likeness view for images
of smell and taste, so too we should reject that view for visual images.

It seems to me that this conclusion is much too hasty. Even if Ryle
is correct in saying that no copy or picture account is appropriate for
imaging smells, it obviously does not follow from this that visual
imagination does not involve any copy or picture. The need for
semantic uniformity in the treatment of statements about visual imagination on the one hand and imagination of smell and taste on the
other could be met by holding that all such statements assert that
the relevant persons are undergoing experiences much like those
normal perceivers undergo in seeing, smelling, or tasting the relevant
objects (whichever is appropriate).[4a] But there is surely no requirement that the *representations* involved in such experiences always be
of the same type. That is a matter to be settled not by armchair
reflection but rather by empirical investigation. It may turn out that
smell representations are in certain respects like visual representations. But whether this is so and what these respects are is something
our ordinary concepts leave open.

A further objection to the picture theory is that it cannot accommodate the vagueness or indeterminacy of many mental images.[5]
This objection has been enormously influential. It has been raised
not just against the picture theory of images but also in parallel form
against the sense-datum theory of visual perception. In one of its
forms, the objection is simply that people sometimes have mental
images or percepts that leave various details out. For example, as I
noted in chapter 1, a person might have a mental image (or a visual
percept) of a tiger and yet be unable to specify how many stripes the
imaged tiger has. This, it is alleged, would not be possible if mental
images (or visual percepts) were pictorial.

The obvious response to the above objection is to point out that
ordinary pictures (e.g., blurred photographs) are sometimes vague
or unclear.[6] However, this response will not refute the more sophisticated versions of the objection. Consider, for example, the views of
Daniel Dennett.[7] Unlike many proponents of the objection from indeterminacy, Dennett acknowledges that pictures can sometimes be
fuzzy. However, according to Dennett, for any visual property P,
you can look at what is pictured by any given picture and determine

whether or not *P* is present, *unless* the relevant portion of the picture is vague or unclear. Dennett maintains that this is not so for mental images. Suppose, for example, I tell you to imagine a woman wearing a red dress. If I then ask you such questions as "Is your imaged woman carrying a handbag?", "What color are her shoes?", and "Does her dress extend below her knees?", you may not be able to say. The problem is not that the relevant portions of your image are obscured. Rather, in Dennett's view, your mental image simply doesn't go into some of the details.

The general point of Dennett's objection, then, can be put in the following way. Imagining, unlike picturing, is subject to a fourfold distinction: it's one thing to imagine an object with visual property *P*; it's another to imagine that object without *P*; it's a third to imagine the object with the relevant portion so obscured that one cannot tell whether *P* is present; and it's a fourth to imagine the object without one's image going into the presence or absence of *P*. By contrast, in the case of picturing, only the first three distinctions are applicable— the fourth is not.

We shall return to this form of the objection from indeterminacy in section 2.3 (and also in chapter 6). For the moment, I want to move on to another, quite different objection to (one version of) the picture theory. This objection—the last I shall mention—has again been highly influential. In its simplest version, it is directed against any theory of mental images that takes images to be physical particulars. Suppose I form a green image. This green image cannot be a physical object, for nothing inside my head is colored green. Nor need there be any green physical object in my immediate environment. Thus, insofar as proponents of the picture theory of images posit physical pictures, they are making a serious mistake. Sometimes this objection is extended further to any theory that takes mental images to be objects, physical or nonphysical. For just as nothing inside my head is colored green, so too, it is sometimes suggested, nothing inside my soul (if I have one) could really be colored green either. Hence, there aren't any mental images at all. Instead, there are merely persons who image in various ways or, alternatively, various acts of imaging.

The above objection was first made by J. J. C. Smart in his famous paper, "Sensations and Brain Processes."[8] The conclusion Smart drew, in his defense of the mind-brain identity theory, was that mental images do not exist. I should add that Smart did not argue against the view that mental images are *nonphysical* particulars in the manner described above. Rather, he was concerned to show that materialism with respect to sensations and imagery is compatible with the ordinary belief that statements like

(1) Smith has a green afterimage

are sometimes true. In Smart's view, (1) is to be analyzed as

(1a) Smith undergoes a visual experience much like the experience he would undergo were he to see a green physical object,

and (1a), in order to be true, does not require the existence of a green image. Hence, materialism is safe.

Is this objection from color successful? I think not. One who wishes to defend the view that mental images are physical particulars can argue that in predicating color words of images, we are doing one of two things: *either* we are using these words elliptically for expressions like "represents (real, objective) green," "represents (real, objective) blue," and so on, *or* we are using them to name intrinsic, phenomenal properties different from (real, objective) color properties. In the former case,[9] there is no difficulty for the view that a green mental image is a neural entity, say, since a neural entity can certainly have some neural quality in virtue of which it *represents* green. In the latter case, again there is no difficulty for the same view, since no argument has been given that neural entities cannot have phenomenal properties. Of course, there are well-known arguments in the literature against the view that phenomenal properties are physical properties. But even if these arguments were sound, there still would be no compelling objection to the view that mental images are physical particulars, that is, particulars that have physical descriptions. For such particulars could still have some nonphysical properties *in addition to* their physical ones.

One other point must be addressed in connection with the objection from color: if color words express intrinsic, phenomenal qualities in application to mental images, as is suggested on one of the two alternatives proposed above, then why are these words used? If phenomenal green isn't real green, then why is it called "green" at all? The answer, I suggest (*if* color words do indeed sometimes express intrinsic, phenomenal qualities),[10] is that in using color terminology, we are making a *conceptual* connection between certain phenomenal qualities and certain colors. Phenomenal green, for example, on one version of this view, is conceived of as the phenomenal quality that is typically caused in normal perceivers by the presence of a green physical object before the eyes. This claim is similar to the one Smart makes in holding that (1) is equivalent to (1a). But there is an important difference (other than the introduction of causal terminology): on the above proposal, there is no denial of the existence of mental images. Thus, (1), for example, is to be taken to assert that *there is* an afterimage that Smith has, and this afterimage has the phenomenal quality typically produced in normal perceivers by viewing green physical objects. The conclusion I draw, then, is that Smart did not need to deny the existence of mental images (or sensory objects generally) in order to save materialism with respect to imagery and sensations.

We have now examined the major twentieth-century philosophical objections to the picture theory of mental images. Some of these objections have been answered; others have been left for a more detailed study in subsequent chapters. In section 2.2, I begin my discussion of the three alternative accounts of imagery that have emerged in philosophy this century.

2.2   *The Behaviorist View of Imagery*

The first alternative to the picture theory that I want to introduce is the behaviorist view of imagery, which began in psychology with J. B. Watson.[11] In Watson's view, mental images are one variety of subvocal thinking. They involve no more than slight movements of the larynx. When one forms a mental image, one is in essence talking to oneself under one's breath. Watson says, for example:

> What then becomes of images? . . . What does a person mean when he closes his eyes or ears (figuratively speaking) and says, "I see the house where I was born, the trundle bed in my mother's room where I used to sleep—I can even see my mother as she comes to tuck me in and I can even hear her voice as she softly says good-night?" Touching, of course, but sheer bunk. We are merely dramatizing. The behaviorist finds no proof of imagery in all this. We have put all these things in words long, long ago and we constantly rehearse those scenes verbally whenever the occasion arises . . . What we mean by being conscious of events which happened in our past is that we can carry on a conversation about them either to ourselves (thought) or with someone else (talk).[12]

In this passage, Watson is not denying the existence of imagery altogether. His point is that people's introspective reports do not demonstrate that there are inner mental *pictures*. Such reports, in Watson's view, merely express opinions, and the opinions they express are badly mistaken. Mental images are really just inner speech.

Work with the drug curare undermines attempts, such as Watson's, to identify mental images with inner, covert behavior. It has been found that patients, treated with sufficient curare to produce complete paralysis of their muscles, report later (when they have recovered) that they were subject to thoughts, sensations, and images during paralysis.

This point—that mental states may be present without covert or overt behavior—is one that behaviorists tried to deal with by appeal to the concept of a behavioral disposition. Even if behavior is not occurring during the presence of the given mental state, still there will be, at that time, a *disposition* to behave in the appropriate way. In philosophy, a view of this sort is associated with Ryle's *The Concept of Mind*. The general thesis of this book is that a satisfactory account of the mental can be given, without invoking inner events or objects, in terms of acquired skills and dispositions to behave in various ways. All psychological states, according to Ryle, are to be understood in terms of witnessable activities rather than in terms of inner, private goings-on. Ryle, then, has generally been classified as a metaphysical or conceptual behaviorist, even though he himself resisted such labels.

In the case of imagery, Ryle's rejection of an inner theater and inner pictures leads him to hold that having a mental image of an *F* (i.e., having a visual image of an *F*) is a matter of seeming to see an *F* or fancying seeing an *F*. Unfortunately, Ryle is far from clear about just what these latter activities involve. His view seems to be that they are to be conceived of as behavioral dispositions, but he offers no clear-cut analysis.

This view of imagery is without any real support in philosophy today. In part, this is due to the decline of behaviorism as a movement in psychology.[13] In part, it is due to the immediate tension between the view and the apparently undeniable fact that imagery does involve *something* inner (whatever its ultimate nature) that is open to introspection. And in part, it is due to the overwhelming difficulties that confront any attempt to analyze image discourse, and indeed any psychological discourse, behavioristically. The underlying general problem, in this last case, is that behavioral responses typically depend upon whole *groups* of mental states. For example, my desiring a glass of champagne causes me to reach for the champagne bottle, but only if I recognize it *as* a champagne bottle, and only if I don't have some other stronger desire that outweighs the first. Thus, any satisfactory definition of a given mental state type *must* take account of its causal connections to other mental state types and hence the behaviorist's definitions are doomed to failure.

2.3   Philosophical Descriptionalism

The second alternative to the picture theory in twentieth-century philosophy is a view commonly known as descriptionalism. This view can be traced back before this century to the passage quoted in chapter 1 from Locke's *Essay Concerning Human Understanding* in which Locke compares the relation between an image and its object to that between a word and what it represents.[14] The view also has some similarity with Watson's claim that imaging is talking to oneself. The basic thesis of descriptionalism is that mental images represent objects in the manner of linguistic descriptions.[15] This thesis should not be taken to imply that during imagery, inner tokens of the imager's spoken language must be present either in the imager's brain or in any movements of the imager's larynx. Rather, the thought is that mental images are neural entities that represent objects in some neural code that is, in important respects, language-like.[16]

Descriptionalism remains popular in philosophy today, and it also has significant support in contemporary psychology.[17] In chapter 4, we shall investigate the empirical data that, some psychologists claim, offer strong evidence for descriptionalism. In the present context, my concern is solely with the *philosophical* underpinnings of the view.

Several factors have influenced the growth of descriptionalism. To begin with, there has been a dissatisfaction with the traditional philosophical reasons for the picture theory and in particular with the appeal to introspection. Descriptionalists would urge, as I did in chapter 1, that all introspection really shows is that having a mental image is experientially rather like seeing. Thus, the question of how objects are represented in mental images (and visual percepts) is left entirely open by the introspective evidence. A second factor in the growth of descriptionalism has been the belief that at least some of the objections canvassed in section 2.1 present insuperable difficulties for the picture theory. A third, and related, factor has been the view that these objections not only present no difficulties for descriptionalism but, in one case at least, actually offer strong support for it. The case I have in mind is that of the objection from indeterminacy. Since descriptions frequently leave things unspecified—I may *say*, for example, that a tiger is approaching or that a man knocked on the door without specifying the number of the tiger's stripes or the presence of a hat on the man's head—it follows that if mental images represent in a descriptional manner, then they too will frequently be representationally indeterminate. This point has been made forcefully by J. M. Shorter[18] and also by Daniel Dennett.[19] The latter has argued further that describing is subject to the same fourfold distinction as imagining. Recall that with respect to imagining, Dennett notes that it is one thing to imagine an object X with visual property P; another to imagine X without P; a third to imagine X with the relevant portion so obscured that one cannot tell whether P is present; and a fourth to imagine X without one's image going into the presence or absence of P. Analogously, it is one thing to say, "X has P"; another to say, "X lacks P"; a third to say, "X is before me but I cannot tell whether X has P," and a fourth to say simply, "X is before me."

It is perhaps worth noting here that there is a worthwhile objection to the view of some descriptionalists that descriptionalism does not face *any* of the standard philosophical puzzles raised in connection with the picture theory at the beginning of section 2.1. If inner pictures require inner eyes to "see" them, so presumably inner descriptions require inner eyes to "read" them. And if descriptions are to be manipulated or altered, then inner hands, scissors, and glue seem necessary also.

It seems to me that the correct descriptionalist response to this argument is to point out that since digital computers "read" and manipulate inner descriptional tokens without "eyes" or "hands" there is no reason to think that we cannot do likewise. In the case of the computer, an account may be given of how it performs a given operation (e.g., multiplication of two numbers) by decomposing it into simpler operations (e.g., addition) repeated an appropriate number of times, until such simple operations are reached that they can only be explained by reference to the hardware of the computer. It is at this level that the software and hardware explanations of the performance of operations come together. What is true here for digital computers is true also for our manipulation of inner descriptional representations, or so the descriptionalist can urge: just as the digital computer handles descriptional representations mechanistically—that is, via mechanisms whose only explanation ultimately is in terms of the computer's hardware (e.g., in terms of electronics)—so too we handle inner representations of the same sort in a corresponding mechanistic manner. Eyes, hands, scissors are not required.[20]

A final factor influencing philosophical descriptionalists has been a desire for theoretical unity.[21] Since memory, belief, desire, and other propositional psychological attitudes are best viewed as being relations to inner sentence tokens, or so many philosophers suppose,[22] a linguistic account of mental images and their representational content yields a more unified approach to the mind overall than does the picture theory.

2.4   The Adverbial Theory and Eliminativism

Let us turn now to the third and last alternative to the picture theory in twentieth-century philosophy. This alternative has two variants, one of which is much more extreme than the other. What unites these two variants is the shared view that there are no mental images. In the case of the less extreme variant, the supporting reasons typically run along the following lines: grammatically, a statement such as

(2) Mary has an image of a red triangle

is on a par with a statement such as

(3) Mary has a red dress.

This grammatical similarity between (2) and (3) suggests a logical similarity too. Thus, just as (3) is to be analyzed as

(3a) There is an object x such that x is a red dress and Mary has x,

so, it is tempting to infer, (2) is to be analyzed as

(2a) There is an object x such that x is an image of a red triangle and Mary has x.

But (2a) generates a whole host of problems and puzzles. Some of these puzzles we have already met in our discussion of objections to the picture theory. And there are others of a more general nature. For example, can there be unowned images (like unowned dresses)? Can two persons have one and the same image (as two persons could jointly own a single dress)? Do mental images have rear surfaces that imagers aren't aware of? If mental images are nonphysical objects, then how did they emerge in the evolution of matter?

What these puzzles suggest is that philosophers, in analyzing (2) as (2a), have been misled by the grammar of ordinary language. Grammatical form is not always a good indicator of logical form. Consider for example, the statement

(4) The average British family has 1.3 children.

The grammatical subject of (4) is "the average British family"; but the logical subject is the number, 1.3, and what (4) really says is that this number is the result of dividing the number of British children by the number of British families. (4), then, does not have the same logical form as (2). Rather, (2) is to be understood in the same general way as

(5) Mary has a noticeable stutter.

In (5), the term "stutter" is a verbal noun. Upon its conversion to a verb, its adjectives become adverbs. Thus, (5) may be rewritten as

(5a) Mary stutters noticeably.

Similarly, (2) is to be analyzed as

(2b) Mary images a-red-triangle-ly.

Of course, (2b) does not yet give us the full logical form of (2). On some accounts, (2b) is analyzed further so as to bring out an ontic commitment to an event of imaging in a certain way, namely, a-red-triangle-ly. On other accounts, (2b) is given a semantics in which "Mary" names Mary, "images" expresses the property of imaging, and "a-red-triangle-ly" is a predicate operator, which, in application to "images," forms another predicate. However the semantic analyses are developed, what is common to these adverbial approaches to imagery is a repudiation of mental images as genuine objects together with an acceptance of the truth of many ordinary, everyday image statements.[23]

This view of imagery, and of sensory experience generally, remains very popular in philosophical circles. Versions of the view are to be found in the writings of, for example, R. M. Chisholm, Wilfrid Sellars, Bruce Aune, and myself.[24] Despite its widespread acceptance, prior to my own publications on the adverbial theory, very little had been said about the semantic and metaphysical foundations of the view. And it is absolutely essential that the semantics and metaphysics be stated clearly. For in the absence of such statements, the adverbial theory may look like a rather trivial grammatical transformation without any real constraints.

The adverbial theory of mental images is not without potential difficulties of its own, however, even putting aside this last point. For *if* it can be shown that ultimately there are clear answers to the (at least initially) puzzling questions faced by theories that take mental images as genuine objects, then there is no immediate reason not to take the grammatical form of image discourse at its face value, in which case the adverbial theory appears to lose one of its major motivations. A second potential difficulty concerns the account that is to be given of representational content. Mental images represent objects. An image of a red triangle is an image that represents a red triangle. How are these facts to be analyzed from an adverbialist perspective? If there are no imagistic representations, then just what has representational content? Further, how is the adverbial approach to be reconciled with work in cognitive psychology on imagery, work that appears to take mental images as objects in their own right?[25]

I come finally to the extreme version of the view that mental images do not exist. This is the eliminativist account favored most notably by Richard Rorty and Paul Churchland.[26] According to eliminativism, the ordinary psychological statements we make from day to day are no more to be trusted than the statements our predecessors made "about" witches, caloric fluid, and phlogiston. Radical error infects the former talk just as it does the latter. Thus, mental events and mental objects generally do not exist, according to the eliminativists, for the simple reason that the everyday statements of our folk psychology are, one and all, false.

What seems to motivate eliminativists is the desire to defend a general materialism together with the belief that any attempt to find neural entities with which to identify mental states at either the token or the type level is fundamentally misguided. In the view of eliminative materialists, psychological discourse has commitments that there is not the slightest reason to think will mesh neatly with our neural hardware.

This version of materialism is very difficult to swallow. One standard objection that carries significant weight with many philosophers is this: if folk psychology is, as a matter of fact, not true, then why does it work so well? Consider, for example, explanations of behavior via beliefs and desires. There can be no denying that the attribution of the appropriate beliefs and desires frequently leads to substantiated behavioral predictions. Why? What accounts for the widespread success of belief-desire psychology? After all, in general isn't predictive success evidence for the truth of a theory, particularly when that theory is without competitors in its own area? Eliminative materialists such as Rorty and Churchland have not satisfactorily answered these questions. Instead, they have focused on what they take to be the "stagnancy" of folk psychology. Their view is that folk psychology is a *bad* theory without *any* successes worth explaining. This strikes many philosophers (myself included) as a decidedly skewed description of the facts.

Another difficulty for eliminativism is the success of theoretical cognitive psychology. Cognitive psychologists are primarily interested in answering "how" questions pertaining to the exercise of our cognitive capacities. They try to explain how we remember, how we understand, how we image, how we perceive, and so on. If none of these cognitive capacities really exist, then it is very difficult to grasp what it is that these psychologists are doing and why it is that at least some of their theories seem to have been so successful.

In conclusion, then, it seems accurate to say that the picture theory of images has lost support among philosophers in part because of its uncritical reliance on introspection and in part because it is plagued by a whole host of objections, several of which are widely considered decisive. Of the alternative views that have emerged to fill the gap left by the repudiation of the picture theory, the adverbial theory and descriptionalism are the most popular, although eliminativism also has some present-day support.

Chapter 3

The Picture Theory in Cognitive Psychology

Despite its unpopularity in contemporary philosophy, the picture theory has become a subject of intense debate in recent cognitive psychology. Some cognitive psychologists, notably Stephen Kosslyn,[1] have argued that the best explanation of a variety of experiments on mental imagery is that mental images are pictorial. Although Kosslyn has valiantly tried to explain just what the basic thesis of the pictorial approach, as he accepts it, amounts to (and he has certainly said much more on this topic than any philosopher), his position remains difficult to grasp. As a result, I believe, it has been badly misunderstood both by prominent philosophers and by prominent cognitive scientists. This seems to me especially unfortunate, since, in my view, Kosslyn's work, once properly elucidated, breathes new life into the moribund body of the picture theory.

The structure of this chapter is as follows. In section 3.1, I present a clear statement of the central thesis of the picture theory, as it is understood by Kosslyn, the foremost contemporary advocate of the theory. I also bring out one alternative way in which the picture theory may be elucidated. In section 3.2, I discuss whether there is really any conflict between the pictorial view of mental images and the digital computer model of the mind, as has been claimed by Ned Block[2] and by Hubert and Stuart Dreyfus,[3] among others. In section 3.3, I briefly summarize the experimental data that allegedly support the picture theory and I show just how the theory explains the data. Finally, in section 3.4, I make some remarks on what imagery is good for from the perspective of the picture theory.

3.1 Kosslyn's Version of the Picture Theory

What can it mean to say that mental images are pictorial? This is no easy question to answer. As I noted earlier, mental images are not really seen. They cannot be hung on real walls. They have no objective weight or color. Moreover, the fact that mental images look like the objects they represent offers no support for the picture theory. Stephen Kosslyn's preliminary response is to propose that mental images are to be conceived of on the model of displays on a cathode ray tube screen attached to a computer. Such displays are generated on the screen by the computer from information that is stored in the computer's memory.

This model, primitive though it is, is superior to certain other pictorialist models. For example, consider the suggestion that mental images are like slides or photographs that are stored in memory and are taken out whenever the experience of imagery occurs. It is evident that this model cannot explain our ability to imagine entirely novel scenes or our ability to add to or alter features of images.

Neither of the above abilities is problematic if we think of images as being like displays on a computer monitor screen, since such displays are *generated* rather than retrieved and they can easily be added to or altered by manipulating the information stored in the computer's memory. But there are obvious differences between mental images and screen displays. So just what are the respects in which the former are supposed to be like the latter?

Kosslyn suggests that before we answer this question, we reflect upon how a picture is formed on a monitor screen and what makes *it* pictorial. We may think of the screen itself as being covered by a matrix in which there are a large number of tiny squares or cells. The pattern formed by placing dots in these cells is pictorial, Kosslyn asserts, because it has spatial features that correspond to spatial features of the represented object.[4] In particular, dots in the matrix represent points on the surface of the object, and relative distance and geometrical relations among dots match the same relations among object points. Thus, if dots A, B, and C in the matrix stand respectively for points P_1, P_2, and P_3 on the object surface, then if P_1 is below P_2 and to P_3's left (as the object is seen from a particular point of view), then likewise A is below B and to C's left (as the screen is seen from a corresponding point of view). Similarly, if P_1 is farther from P_2 than from P_3, then A is farther from B than from C.

It is perhaps worth noting that this last claim needs qualification if it is to be generally applicable. For P_1 may be farther from P_2 than from P_3 on the object surface and yet appear to be closer to P_2 within the context of the relevant point of view. It would be more accurate to say, then, that if P_1 *appears* farther from P_2 than from P_3 (relative to the relevant point of view), then A is farther from B than from C.[5] A qualification of this sort is also needed in Kosslyn's claim concerning geometrical relations.

Kosslyn's reasoning now becomes more opaque. The main strand of thought in Kosslyn's writings seems to be that although mental images lack the above spatial characteristics, they nonetheless function *as if* they had those characteristics. Thus, in Kosslyn's view, it is not literally true that mental images are pictures. Rather, the truth in the picture theory is that mental images are *functional* pictures.

But just what is involved in something's being a functional picture (or a "quasi-picture," as Kosslyn sometimes says)? Kosslyn's discussion of this pressing question is not easy to follow. In *Ghosts in the Mind's Machine*, Kosslyn presents an example to illuminate what he has in mind. Here is the example (with minor modifications).[6] Suppose a cross figure is drawn in a 7 × 7 matrix as in figure 3.1. Suppose now that 49 different people are each shown figure 3.1 and are each told to memorize whether a given square is filled, with different squares being assigned to different people. The information that is in figure 3.1 is now also stored in the group of 49 people. If you later meet this group of people and ask whether square (1,1) is filled, whether square (1,2) is filled, and so on through the whole matrix, you can reconstruct from their responses—either the single word "filled" or silence—what is pictured in figure 3.1. This group of people—or more precisely their collective positive responses—forms a functional picture, according to Kosslyn. He says:

> Even though the people may be standing anywhere, they [can] function to represent points that are close together in the matrix, diagonal, and so on. All the information in the picture is available, even though there is no actual picture.[7]

It is, I think, evident that this example does *not* really clarify what makes something a functional picture and hence that Kosslyn's pic-

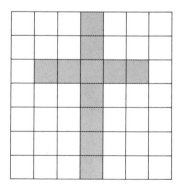

Figure 3.1

ture theory remains obscure. I want now to try to remove this obscurity. Later I shall return to Kosslyn's example, and I shall show why the positive replies of the group of people form a functional picture, as Kosslyn asserts.

According to Kosslyn, spatial structure plays a central role in pictorial representation. To arrive at a significant thesis, I suggest that Kosslyn needs some way of exploiting this view without thereby being forced into the extreme position that mental images are genuine, realistic pictures.

It seems to me that one possible model in this context is presented by the retinotopic representations found on the visual cortex in visual perception. These retinotopic representations reconstruct the retinal image in the cortex. However, the retinal surface is not reconstructed in a linear manner. Rather, the image is distorted as if it had been printed on a sheet of rubber, which had then been irregularly stretched. Consider, then, the case of a pictorial pattern of a single object O imprinted on rubber. After the rubber has been stretched in all directions in varying degrees, many of the pattern's internal spatial relations (for example, its components' relative distance relations) will change dramatically, and the pattern as a whole will no longer be a realistic picture. Nonetheless, any path drawn on the rubber prior to stretching and divided into segments retains the same number of segments after stretching even though their lengths change. Moreover, both before and after stretching, every part of the rubber that represents anything represents a part of the represented object O.

Reflection upon these facts suggests to me a general analysis of quasi-picturing along the following lines:

> A representation R is a quasi-picture of an object O as seen from point of view V if, and only if, (i) every part of R that represents anything represents a part of O visible from V; (ii) a sufficient number of apparent relative surface distance relationships among parts of O visible from V are represented in R; (iii) for any three represented O parts, X, Y, and Z, if X appears at a greater surface distance from Y than from Z, then this fact is represented in R if and only if there are more R parts representing apparently adjacent O parts that are connected by the shortest apparent path on the surface of O between X and Y and that are each of the same apparent length L as measured along that path than there are R parts representing the corresponding O parts of apparent length L between X and Z.[7a]

Some comments are necessary on this proposal: (1) Insofar as an analysis is being offered, it is an analysis of what makes a given representation (of O) *quasi-pictorial* and not an analysis of what makes something a *quasi-pictorial representation* (of O). Thus, although my proposal uses the concept of representation, there is no circularity resulting from this usage. In this chapter, I shall have nothing to say about the concept of representation in general. (2) Condition (i) is included in the analysis on the assumption that R is a quasi-picture of O and of no other object that is not an undetached part of O. If R is a quasi-picture of O together with certain other objects (that are not parts of O), condition (i) will be too strong and should be replaced by the following condition: The part of R that represents O has representational parts, each of which represents a part of O visible from V. (3) In those cases where a representation R meets the three stated conditions without the restrictions about point of view and appearance, R may be said to be a quasi-picture of O without adding the qualification "as seen from point of view V." (4) If we want to say that quasi-picturing admits of degrees so that some representations are very minimal quasi-pictures whereas others are strongly quasi-pictorial, we will need to replace the phrase "a sufficient number" in (ii) by some such term as "few" or "numerous," whichever is appropriate to the given degree of quasi-picturing. (5) The stated analysis applies to the case of quasi-pictorial representation of one given object. It is not intended to cover what it is for a representation to be a quasi-picture of an object of type F (though no one object of that type in particular). (6) The notion of part at work in the analysis requires some comment. It seems to me that there is good reason to deny that either O parts or R parts must be natural. To see this, consider a skeletal map of the United States. Suppose that on this map there is a dot representing Chicago, a dot representing Los Angeles, and a dot representing New York, and that nothing other than the United States boundaries is marked. Would this map be a quasi-picture of the United States? If the representational parts of the map are taken to be bits of ink spatially located within its perimeter, then the answer is no, for greater distances among parts of the United States represented by dots (i.e., cities) are nowhere represented via greater numbers of dots. However, if the representational parts are taken to include arbitrary unmarked regions within the map's perimeter, then the answer is yes. Let me explain.

The only cities represented on the map are Chicago, Los Angeles, and New York. Nonetheless, it seems reasonable to say that other parts of the United States are also represented, if O parts and R parts can be arbitrary as well as natural. For example, the western half of the United States is represented by the left half of the map (within the boundary lines); the lower third of the United States is represented by the lower third of the map; and so on. Imagine now a straight path drawn between the dot representing Chicago and the dot representing Los Angeles. Imagine further that this path is arbitrarily divided into four segments, each of the same length (one inch, say). Then it seems reasonable to hold that the region of the map making up the first such segment connected to the dot representing Chicago represents a region of the United States that ends at Chicago and that has a certain length (500 miles, say) and a certain breadth (appropriate to the width of the imaginary path). The second segment represents an adjacent region of the same size. Similarly the third and fourth. Since there will be more of these one-inch segments between the dots representing Chicago and Los Angeles than between the dots representing Chicago and New York, the fact that Chicago is farther from Los Angeles than from New York will be represented in the map in the manner required by condition (iii) (ignoring the irrelevant qualifications about appearance and points of view). And many other relative distance relations between arbitrary parts of the United States or its boundaries will also be similarly represented. The map will therefore count as a quasi-picture, according to the stated proposal. What makes the map described above different from most quasi-pictures is the fact that the parts of it that represent adjacent parts of the same size are themselves physically adjacent and also of the same size so that greater distances among parts of the represented entity (in this case the United States) are represented via greater distances on the representation. As I noted earlier, this feature is found in genuine realistic pictures (given the qualification I stated). But it is certainly not required for quasi-pictures, as defined above.

My suggestion, then, is that we should permit the term "part" in my account to apply to both arbitrary and natural parts. Now not all parts of a representation R need be representational any more than all parts of the object O need be represented. Two questions may thus be distinguished: "What makes a given R part (or any entity for that matter) representational?" and "What makes a given R part a part of R?" Though I shall have nothing to say on the general concept of representation in this chapter, I do want to make some brief remarks in response to the second question. It seems to me that a very natural requirement to impose on R parts is that they be spatially within R as a whole. Such an interpretation of "R part" rules out the possibility that mental images are nonphysical quasi-pictures and indeed that there are any nonphysical quasi-pictures at all. However, this consequence is one that few philosophers or psychologists would find unpalatable. Moreover, the above interpretation does not place *severe* restrictions on the physical realization of mental images, for it does not preclude quasi-pictures from having widely scattered parts. Still, it does entail that every R part be assigned a smaller region in space than R or any part of R of which it is a part. And some pictorialists may want to argue that even this consequence is too strong, that further latitude is desirable in the physical realization of mental images on the pictorialist hypothesis. Likewise, some descriptionalists may want to deny that their talk of representational parts commits them to the view that such parts *must* be spatially within the representations of which they are parts. Anyone who takes this line must show that it makes sense to suppose that the parts of a representation include abstract functional parts that are not necessarily spatial parts. If this can be done, then my talk of R parts need not be tied to a spatial interpretation of the term "part."[8]

Now the proposal we have arrived at not only has some continuity with Kosslyn's view of the way in which a display on a monitor screen is genuinely pictorial but also unifies and sharpens a number of other statements that Kosslyn makes, statements such as the following:

> The primary characteristic of representations in this format [that is, quasi-pictures] is that every portion of the representation must correspond to a portion of the object such that the relative interportion distances on the object are preserved by the distances among the corresponding portions of the representation.[9]

> Importantly, distance in the medium [of quasi-pictorial representation] can be defined without reference to actual physical distance but merely in terms of the number of locations intervening between any two locations.[10]

Furthermore, we can understand why Kosslyn holds that the positive answers of the 49 people in the example cited earlier form a functional picture of the cross figure in figure 3.1. Given the context provided by the questions, Kosslyn takes each token of the term "filled" to represent a cross figure part. These tokens are themselves representationally simple. Hence, the scattered entity—call it "S"—composed of these tokens has no representational parts that do not represent parts of the cross figure. Hence, S meets condition (i).[11] S also meets both conditions (ii) and (iii) without the qualifications about point of view and appearance, assuming we agree that a sufficient number of relative surface distance relations among parts of the cross figure are represented in S, as condition (ii) requires. Hence, S is a functional picture of the cross figure. By contrast, a description such as "the cross-shaped figure in figure 3.1" or "the figure composed of 11 darkened squares located within the central column and the third row from the top in the diagram on page 35" would not be a functional picture of the cross figure, since none of the conditions (i)–(iii) is met. Not even a list that expressed in written sentences of the form "Square (n,k) is filled" the information that is conveyed by all the positive oral responses of the people would qualify as a functional picture of the cross figure. This is because such a list does not meet condition (i): there are representationally complex parts of the list (e.g., "(3,2) is filled") whose component representational parts (e.g., "2," "3," "is filled") do not represent parts of the cross figure (but rather represent numbers and the property of being filled). Hence, although quasi-pictures are not full-fledged realistic pictures, they nonetheless represent in a different way than either sentences or descriptions. Hence, Kosslyn cannot be charged with taking a view of mental imagery that does not provide a significant *alternative* to the view of Pylyshyn and other descriptionalists.

Various passages in Kosslyn's writings suggest that Kosslyn often has a more restrictive understanding of the notion of a quasi-picture than the one supplied above.[12] In these passages, it seems clear that a quasi-picture is supposed to be employed in a picture-like representational way by the cognitive system of which it is a part. That is, not only is the representation taken to have a picture-like structure vis-à-vis the object it represents, but it is also taken to be subject to processing, within the given cognitive system, that is *suitably structure-sensitive*. Let me elaborate on this point.

Pictures, like maps, can be used to determine the presence or absence of a variety of different spatial relationships among parts of the items they represent, for example, whether parts A, B, and C fall on a straight line, whether they are adjacent, whether A is farther from B than from C. Quasi-pictures, on the present understanding, in virtue of being quasi-pictures, are subject to processing that is sensitive to their internal representational structure and that thereby enables the cognitive systems of which they are parts to treat them *as if* they were pictures with respect to such uses. On this reading of Kosslyn, we may propose the following analysis of quasi-picturing in place of the first one:

> A representation R is a quasi-picture of an object O as seen from point of view V for person P or system S if, and only if, (i) the three conditions in the first definition are satisfied; (ii) there are

processes within P or S that operate upon the parts of R in a way that results in their functioning with respect to the determination of a variety of spatial relationships among parts of O as they would were they parts of a real picture of O as seen from V.

This definition seems to me compatible with the general framework of Kosslyn's position.

One further aspect of Kosslyn's conception of the picture theory must still be introduced. Consider again a cathode ray tube screen on which a picture is displayed. The screen may be thought of as the medium in which the picture is presented. This medium is spatial, and it is made up of a large number of basic units or cells, some of which are illuminated to form a picture. Analogously, according to Kosslyn, there are various functional spatial media, each made up of a number of basic units or cells.[13] These units or cells may be active or not. For example, in the case of the represented cross figure, the functional spatial medium is made up of the 49 responses. Those responses that are positive, that is, those that token the word "filled" in answer to a question, are the active units in the functional medium. Those responses that are silent are the inactive units. Each of the former responses, by virtue of being active, represents the presence of a filled square at a particular spatial location in figure 3.1.

We are now ready to state the *basic* thesis of the only picture theory of imagery that has been worked out in any detail: mental images exist in a medium that functions as a space; they are themselves functional pictures in this medium. Kosslyn hypothesizes that the imagery medium, which he calls the "visual buffer," is shared with perception.[14] In veridical perception, any given unit in the medium, by being active, represents the presence of a just noticeable object part at a particular spatial location within the field of view. In imagery, the same unit, by being active, represents the very same thing. Thus, imaged object parts are represented within an image as having certain viewpoint-relative locations they do not in fact occupy, namely, those locations they would have occupied in the field of view had the same object parts produced the same active units during normal vision. Kosslyn hypothesizes further that the visual buffer is roughly circular in shape. What he means by this hypothesis is not that the buffer is *literally* circular but rather that if all its component cells were active, the object represented would be circular (or at least would appear to be circular). Admittedly, Kosslyn is not very clear on this point or on certain other characteristics of the visual buffer (and the images formed in it). For example, he often speaks as if his theory requires that represented relative distances actually obtain between the appropriate image parts. These ways of speaking have caused considerable confusion. But the fault lies at least partially with Kosslyn's readers. For there is no more reason to take such talk literally than there is to take literally our everyday ascription of colors to mental images. In speaking of an image as green, say, as I noted in chapter 2, we are not asserting that it has the real color green. Rather, we are saying that it has a quality that *represents* that color. And what is true here for colors is true mutatis mutandis for relative distances.

Another illustration of this point is found in the application of words like "loud" or "high-pitched" to graphical representations of sounds. As Ned Block has noted,[15] it is commonplace for people who work with oscilloscope readings to use such terms in connection with the readings themselves. In this usage it is obvious that what "loud" and "high-pitched" really mean are "represents loud" and "represents high-pitched" respectively.

Kosslyn postulates that there are three basic types of processes that operate on images in the visual buffer, namely, those that "generate," "inspect," and "transform" the images. The generation process acts on information stored in long-term memory about the appearances of objects and their spatial structure, and, from this, it creates an image in the buffer. We are not conscious of the information in long-term memory on which the generation process acts. Rather, what we consciously experience is the pattern of activation that results in the visual buffer. On Kosslyn's view, the generation process itself is decomposable into further processes; but these need not concern us now. The inspection process is also really a number of different processes that examine patterns of activated cells in the buffer, thereby enabling us to recognize shapes, spatial configurations, and other characteristics of the imaged objects. For example, if I form an image of a racehorse, it is the inspection process that allows me to decide whether the tip of its tail extends below its rear knees. Similarly, if I image the Star of David by mentally superimposing two triangles, the inspection process is what enables me to recognize the hexagon in the middle.[16] Finally, there are transformation processes. These processes "rotate," "scale in size," or "translate" the patterns of activated cells in the buffer. I shall have more to say about image transformations in section 3.3.

That, then, in outline is Kosslyn's theory. The overall structure of his position may be diagrammed as shown in figure 3.2.

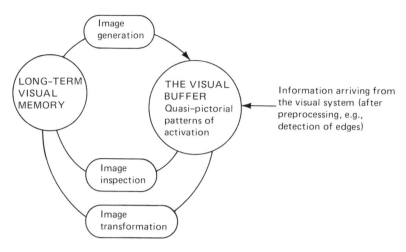

Figure 3.2
The basic components of Kosslyn's theory

Before I close this section, I want to mention one alternative way in which the picture theory could be developed. This gives us a more robust version of the view that mental images are picture-like.

Consider again the retinotopic representations. One fact about these representations that is not utilized within the earlier analysis of quasi-picturing is that, in a quite literal sense, adjacent parts represent adjacent parts of the retinal image. There is, then, an orderly topographic projection of the retinal image onto the visual cortex. We know this from experiments in which a recording electrode is placed inside the cortex. Greater neural activity is picked up by the electrode when light is shined onto a particular spot on the retina. Moving the electrode a little results in the continued registration of greater activity only if light is directed onto an adjacent part of the retina.

Topographic organization of this sort is found in many brain areas. For example, in the somatosensory cortex there is an orderly representation of the surface of the human body that is structured in the same general way. Here adjacent regions of the body surface are projected onto adjacent regions of the cortex. Enhanced activity in one of the relevant cortical regions indicates that the region of body surface projected onto it is being touched. Some relatively small portions of the body (e.g., the hands and face) provide input to more neurons than do some relatively large portions (e.g., the trunk). Thus, when people are asked whether two separate points are being touched on their faces or just one, the smallest interval at which they can feel both points is much less than the smallest interval when the points are located on the trunk. In the motor cortex, the body surface is projected in much the same way as in the somatosensory cortex, the main difference being that now enhanced activity in a cortical region represents movement in a corresponding region of the bodily surface. Since the hands and face are projected more fully than other body parts, it is not surprising that the finest movements we are capable of making involve our hands and faces.

The fact that neurons in different regions of the brain are organized into topographic representations like those described above naturally leads to the conjecture that the imagery system itself employs such representations. If this is so, then it seems to me there will be a more robust sense in which mental images are quasi-pictorial than I have so far admitted. Let me explain.

Instead of the first definition of a quasi-picture, we might now propose the following account:

> A representation R is a quasi-picture of an object O as seen from point of view V, if, and only if, (i) every part of R that represents anything represents a part of O visible from V; (ii) a sufficient number of apparent adjacency relationships among parts of O visible from V are represented in R; (iii) any apparent adjacency relationship among parts of O that is represented in R is represented in such a manner that the parts of R representing those O parts are (literally) adjacent to one another.

I have ignored here the later requirement that quasi-pictures be employed in a picture-like way by the cognitive system of which they are parts solely to simplify my statement of the new proposal. Obviously, this requirement may easily be added to the three conditions formulated above.

The comments (1)—(5) made with respect to the first proposal still apply. As far as comment (6) goes, there is one change: since the above definition obviously entails that every R part that represents anything is spatially within R as a whole, the notion of "part" at work *must* now be understood spatially. There is one further comment I want to make on the new proposal. Condition (iii) is stated in such a way that it does not entail that any two adjacent R parts represent apparently adjacent parts of the represented object. This is because there could be a quasi-picture (e.g., a crumpled rubber sheet on which a picture is drawn) that has some adjacent representational parts that do not represent apparently adjacent parts of the object (see figure 3.3).

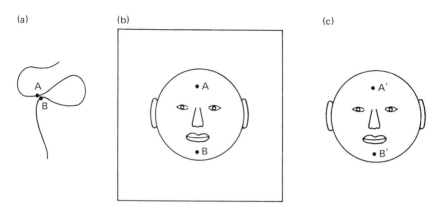

Figure 3.3
(a) Crumpled sheet (side view). *A* is adjacent to *B*. (b) Uncrumpled sheet. *A* is not adjacent to *B*. (c) Represented face. *A'* is not adjacent to *B'*. (*A* represents *A'*; *B* represents *B'*.)

It seems to me entirely reasonable to maintain that any item that is a quasi-picture in the sense just elucidated is picture-like in important ways. Furthermore, any such item will count as a quasi-picture in the first sense. The converse, however, is not true. For example, the oral representation consisting of the positive responses of the 49 people will not pass the new condition (iii), since the people can stand wherever they please. Thus, the new definition gives us a more robust concept of quasi-picturing than did the first one. As a result, the hypothesis that mental images are quasi-pictures is now bolder than before and therefore more vulnerable to empirical refutation.

3.2   The Picture Theory and the Digital Computer Model of the Mind

It is often supposed that Kosslyn's picture theory is inconsistent with the digital computer model of the mind. For example, Ned Block says the following:

> If the pictorialist view is right, then the human brain deploys representations (and processes operating over them) of a sort not found in digital computers (whose representations are paradigms of descriptional representations). So digital computers would not be able to process information in the manner of humans (though of course they might nonetheless be able to simulate human information processing).[17]

Elsewhere, Block asserts:

> The relevance of the pictorial/descriptional controversy to the viability of the computer metaphor in cognitive science should be becoming visible. The computer metaphor goes naturally with descriptional representations, but it is not at all clear how it can work when the representations are nondescriptional.[18]

Similarly, Hubert and Stuart Dreyfus comment:

> [C]omputers, programmed as logic machines, cannot use images or any picturelike representations without transforming them into descriptions.[19]

These statements reflect a serious misunderstanding of Kosslyn's picture theory. Block and the Dreyfus brothers assume that within digital computers there are no picture-like representations. But this is not what Kosslyn himself thinks. For example, Kosslyn makes the following statements about functional pictures:

> [They] can only exist in a medium that functions as a space. . . . The space can be a physical one (such as a piece of paper or a television screen) or a functional one (such as a matrix in a computer's memory).[20]

> [T]here is no physical matrix—actual glass screen—inside a computer on which pictures are displayed; rather, cells in a hypothetical matrix are represented as entries in the machine's memory. The computer identifies these elements in a way that results in their functioning as if they were arranged in a visual array.[21]

But *how* can a digital computer contain functional pictures? The thought that there is a difficulty here rests, I think, on something like the following line of reasoning: Suppose that the responses of the 49 people in the earlier example are translated into ordered combinations of numbers, for example, "*n,k*,1" and "*n,k*,0," where the first of the three numbers indicates row, the second indicates column, and the final "1" or "0" represents whether or not the square is filled. A list of these combinations of numbers can be entered into a computer's memory, and the information stored may be used to generate a picture on the computer's display screen. Now this list is made up of descriptional representations. Hence, it is difficult to see how, as Kosslyn supposes, there can be a functional picture of the cross figure *inside* the computer that is not itself descriptional.

This line of reasoning is seductive but fallacious. Let me explain. I shall focus initially on the first definition of functional picturing. A list of coordinates stored in a file on a computer disk, a list made up of descriptional equivalents of sentences of the forms "Square (n,k) is filled" and "Square (n,k) is empty," admittedly does not itself have members that together form a functional picture, since it is evident that condition (i) in the initial definition is not met. However, if the computer is running a program that requires it to access this file in such a way that somewhere else inside the computer, for each of the above descriptional representations of the form "Square (n,k) is filled," a certain inner cell is actually filled (e.g., by charging electrically a certain physical region), then there will be an inner functional picture made up of these filled cells (charged regions), assuming that conditions (ii) and (iii) in the first definition are met as well as condition (i). Thus, the crucial distinction is between, on the one hand, the sentences we use to describe various filled cells or the sentences the computer uses to identify certain cells to be filled and, on the other hand, the cells so described or identified.

The above computer example is not purely hypothetical. Digital computers used for graphics contain (and manipulate) both descriptional and functional-pictorial representations, the former making up unstructured lists on files, the latter being located in what are known as "arrays." The Appendix contains a simple program that requires setting up internal arrays for the purposes of rotating a line and displaying the rotation on a monitor screen.[22] Thus, Kosslyn's pictorialism (as I initially elucidated it) really poses no threat to the digital computer model of the mind. Indeed, the contrary is the case.

Is there any threat to the digital computer model, if pictorialism is elucidated in the stronger ways connected with the second and third definitions at the end of section 3.1? Again, it seems to me that there is not. As far as the second definition goes, it is unproblematic to suppose that there can be suitable structure-sensitive processing of the appropriate representational structures within digital computers. The contents of internal arrays can be scanned and rotated, for example, in the very same incremental ways that Kosslyn hypothesizes quasi-pictures generally can be scanned and rotated.[23]

In the case of the final definition, we need only realize that the cells in an internal array that are treated by the computer via its program as adjacent *could* be realized physically by machine parts that are literally adjacent to one another, although, of course, typically the relevant machine parts will be physically separated. On the computational model, then, there is nothing to *preclude* the relevant parts from being physically adjacent: it's just that if they are, their being so does no direct representational work. What matters to the representation of adjacency via cells of an internal array is that the program be such that the appropriate cells are identified *as if* they were adjacent to one another. I conclude that the hypothesis that mental images are quasi-pictures can be accommodated within the digital computer model.

3.3   The Experimental Evidence for Kosslyn's Account

Kosslyn and his fellow workers have marshaled a very large quantity of empirical evidence in support of their position. In this section, I shall review some of this evidence. Let me begin with the claim that vision and imagery share a common fixed medium. If there really is a shared medium utilized in both seeing and imaging, then there should be interference effects between the two. This is indeed the case. For example, in one experiment subjects were shown figure 3.4 and asked to image it. They were then told to image the star moving clockwise around the letter and to use their image to decide whether each corner of the imaged letter that the star passed was attached to an upper edge. One group of subjects was told to say yes if the corner was so attached and no otherwise. For this group, then, the correct answers were no, yes, yes, no, no, yes, yes, no, no, no. A second group of subjects was told to give their responses by pointing at a Y or an N on a blackboard resembling figure 3.5. In this case, then, the subjects had to search visually for a response at the same time that they were inspecting their images. It was found that the

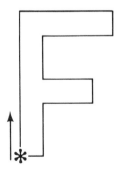

Figure 3.4
Reprinted, by permission, from L. R. Brooks, "Spatial and Verbal Components of the Act of Recall," *Canadian Journal of Psychology* 22 (1968), pp. 349–368. Copyright 1968. Canadian Psychological Association.

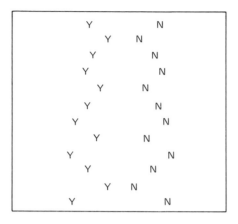

Figure 3.5

second task took much longer—just what one would expect if there is a common medium.

In another experiment, subjects were shown patterns of black vertical stripes against a red background and black horizontal stripes against a green background. They looked at these patterns for 10 minutes, switching back and forth between the two. They were then presented with a pattern of black vertical and horizontal stripes against a white background. The subjects reported that the vertical stripes were tinged with green and the horizontal ones were tinged with red. This effect is known as the "McCollough effect." A similar effect is obtained with imagery. In this case, subjects were shown a red patch and asked to imagine black vertical stripes on it. They were also shown a green patch and asked to imagine black horizontal stripes. They did this alternately for 10 minutes. They were then shown the same black-and-white pattern as before. The same effect resulted, although the colors were reported to be generally fainter. This strongly suggests that at least some of the same mechanisms are at play in both imagery and perception.[24] Shared mechanisms are a central feature of Kosslyn's theory—in addition to a common medium, there are also common inspection procedures.

Here are three further experiments that support the claim of shared mechanisms. Roger Shepard showed a group of subjects a matrix and asked them to imagine a letter in it by mentally blacking in certain areas.[25] A dot or dots were then placed in the matrix, and the subjects were asked whether the dot or dots fell on the imaged letter. The experiment was then repeated with a real letter in the matrix instead of an imaged one. It was found that in both cases the relative response times were the same. For example, when a single dot was placed off the letter, the farther away from the letter it was, the faster the decision was reached. When more than one dot fell on the letter, again a faster response was given.

The second experiment involved stroke victims suffering from a condition known as "unilateral visual neglect." These people have great difficulty in seeing objects on one side of their visual field. For example, if a finger is wiggled on both sides of their visual field simultaneously, they will report seeing only one of the two wigglings. They do *see* both finger movements, however: if only a single finger is wiggled, they will report seeing it (whichever side it is on). People with this defect duplicate it in imagery. For example, an Italian man was asked to image a favorite piazza and to describe the buildings in it using his image. In his description, he systematically ignored all the features of the buildings on the right side of the piazza relative to his imagined point of view.[26]

The third experiment required subjects to briefly view a pattern (e.g., the Star of David) and then, after its removal, to judge whether some simpler subpattern had been present. The subjects responded by generating an image and inspecting it for the relevant part. It was found that certain subpatterns were discovered faster than others, namely, those that were "good" subpatterns in the Gestalt sense, just as in the perceptual case. For example, the parallelogram facing right was harder to pick out than the two main triangles in mental images of the Star of David (see figure 3.6). The main difference between the case of imaging and the case of seeing a pattern was the speed of the answers. In imagery, the answers took longer. This fact does not undermine Kosslyn's claim that common recognitional procedures are at work. Rather, it suggests that factors in addition

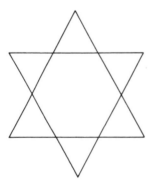

Figure 3.6

to the Gestalt laws of organization are relevant. One possibility proposed by Kosslyn himself is that sustaining an image requires effort, so that it is harder to inspect an image than a pattern on paper. This possibility fits in well with the results of other experiments that indicate that more time is required to "see" portions of more complex images. For if images begin to fade as soon as they are generated in the visual buffer, more complex images will be harder to sustain and all images must be refreshed with new parts, if they are not to disappear.

In Kosslyn's view, then, imagery and perception share various inspection processes and the same medium.[27] I turn next to the evidence that is supposed to support Kosslyn's claims concerning the structure of this medium.[28] In one experiment, subjects were told to form an image of an object in the distance and to imagine themselves walking toward it. They were then asked whether there was a point at which not all of the object could be seen. They all answered affirmatively. Kosslyn takes this result to show that the visual buffer has a limited spatial extent. What he means by this claim is really that the visual buffer has a limited number of basic representational units or parts. Initially, that is, when the object is imaged in the distance, not all of the units in the medium are active. As the object is imaged at closer range, however, more units become active, each one representing a small part of the object visible from the relevant point of view, until eventually all the units are active and the object fills the image, so to speak. From here on, imaging the object any closer requires the imager to leave out parts of the object. Thus, the object "overflows" the image. The same result occurs in perception, of course. As one walks toward an object one is seeing, the object eventually "overflows" one's visual field. The fact that imagery is like seeing in this respect does not itself suffice to explain image "overflow." One can still ask what it is about seeing that generates "overflow" there, to which Kosslyn's response is, "A medium with a limited spatial extent."

In another experiment, subjects were shown a 1-foot ruler horizontally mounted on a wall at eye level. They were then told to image the ruler as shown and to imagine walking toward it. At the point at which the ends of the imaged ruler began to "overflow" from their image, they were asked to estimate how far away from the wall they would have been, had they been viewing the ruler with their eyes and had it appeared just as in their image. The experiment was repeated with the ruler in the vertical position and then again with the ruler at 45 degrees. It was found that the distance estimates were roughly the same in all three cases. Kosslyn says that this shows that the visual buffer is roughly circular in shape. This claim is not to be taken literally, as I noted earlier. What Kosslyn really means is that when all the units in the buffer are active, a circular object or an apparently circular object will be represented. Just how does Kosslyn reach this conclusion? He doesn't say. Presumably the reasoning goes as follows: Assuming an imagery medium with a limited number of units, in imagining oneself walking toward the horizontal ruler, one is activating more and more units representing visible ruler parts. At the point of "overflow," all the units available for representing horizontal object parts will be active. What the data show is that the same number of units are active at this point whether the ruler is horizontal, vertical, or at 45 degrees. It follows that if all the units are simultaneously active, an object will be represented that is the same apparent length in all three directions—that is, a circular (or apparently circular) object—assuming, of course, that similar results are found for other intermediate directions.

Kosslyn also claims that the imagery medium has a grain. Here Kosslyn is to be understood as asserting that the medium has basic representational parts that cannot represent object parts smaller than a certain size, as seen from a certain distance. This is shown, Kosslyn thinks, by experiments in which subjects take longer to see subjectively smaller parts of images. For example, when subjects imaged a rabbit next to an elephant, they took longer to see the rabbit's whiskers clearly than when they imaged a rabbit next to a fly. In the former case, Kosslyn claims that the rabbit's head initially appeared too small for its whiskers to be clearly represented in the subjects' images. Therefore, the subjects employed a "zooming in" process that transformed the image part representing the rabbit's head until it appeared large enough for the whiskers to be clearly visible.

Kosslyn maintains that the resolution in the imagery medium decreases toward the periphery. The experiment in this case required subjects to inspect visually a pair of small dots located in the center of a blank field. The dots were then removed, and the subjects imagined that they were still present. Next the subjects imagined that their focus of attention was moving away from the dots until they could no longer tell that the dots were separate. It was found that the greater the distance between the pair of dots, the farther from the center of the image field the dots could still be resolved. A parallel result was obtained in the perceptual case. On Kosslyn's view, this demonstrates that the basic representational units in the visual buffer represent larger regions toward the periphery, so that resolution there is not as good as in the center. As Kosslyn puts it,

"In the highly resolved central regions the grain is smaller and hence resolution higher."[29]

Why should this be so? One explanation that seems to me rather plausible is this: Since the receptive fields on the retina become larger and correspondingly less sensitive with increasing distance from the fovea, the visual buffer needs to be most highly resolved with respect to material in the central regions of the field of view. Again there is a parallel with the retinotopic representations. Here there is a larger proportion of the cortex devoted to the projection of the foveal area of the retina than elsewhere. Why? Because there is a greater density of photoreceptors around the fovea.

I turn next to the experiments on mental image scanning.[30] In Kosslyn's well-known map-scanning experiment, subjects were required to study the map shown in figure 3.7. When the subjects had become familiar enough with the map to be able to draw it, they were asked to form a mental image of it and then to focus on one particular object in the image. This request was repeated for different objects. It was found that the farther away an object was from the place on the image presently being focused on, the longer it took to focus on that new object. For example, shifting attention from the "lake part" of the image to the "hut part" took longer than shifting attention from the "well part" to the "hut part."

In another experiment performed by Ronald Finke and Steven Pinker, subjects were shown a pattern made up of dots on a screen.[31] The pattern was removed, and the subjects were told to form an image of it just as it had been on the screen. An arrow was then flashed, which, in half the trials, pointed to a previous location of a dot. Subjects were asked whether there was an imagined dot toward which the arrow pointed. When the arrow pointed to where a real dot had been, it was found that the time taken to answer increased linearly with the distance between the tip of the arrow and the dot.

Pictorialists take these experiments to show that mental images can be scanned at fixed speeds. How exactly does this hypothesis explain the results? After all, on the pictorial view, images are not so constituted that their parts bear the same relative distance relations to one another as the object parts they represent. The answer goes as follows: Scanning across a mental image involves accessing the appropriate image parts serially (either by shifting the locus of attention across a stationary image or by translating the imaged pattern across the visual buffer so that different aspects of the pattern fall under a fixed central focus of attention). More specifically, in the map case, scanning across the image involves accessing one after another the members of a sequence of representationally simple im-

Figure 3.7
Kosslyn's map figure. Reprinted, by permission, from S. M. Kosslyn, S. Pinker, G. E. Smith, and S. P. Shwartz, "On the Demystification of Mental Imagery," in *Imagery*, ed. by Ned Block (Cambridge, Mass.: MIT Press, 1981).

age parts, each of which represents a different, just noticeable location on the map situated on a line connecting the figures represented at the beginning and end of scanning. Thus, if the image has parts A, B, and C that represent respectively map parts X, Y, and Z, and X is nearer to Y than to Z, then scanning across the image from A to B will involve successively accessing fewer image parts than scanning from A to C. Thus, assuming a fixed scanning speed, Kosslyn's view predicts that the time it takes to scan from A to B will be shorter than the time it takes to scan from A to C. And this is indeed the result we get.

There may seem to be a tension between the account just offered of image scanning and Kosslyn's claim that the resolution of the visual buffer is such that its representationally simple parts represent larger material regions toward the periphery. For if the just noticeable map parts vary in size according to their position in the field of view, there will be cases where the number of image parts scanned does not increase linearly with the real distance on the map. The experiments on resolution, however, suggest that it is only rather close to the periphery that resolution diminishes significantly. Since, in the scanning experiments cited above, there is no scanning in peripheral regions, the changes in resolution in the buffer play no role. With respect to the operation of the scanning process in the above cases, Kosslyn takes the view that it consists in translating the image pattern across the buffer so that new aspects fall under a fixed central focus of attention.[32] On this model, the buffer parts or units systematically change their activation levels during the scanning process. This is illustrated in figure 3.8. Thus, the parts of the buffer that are being

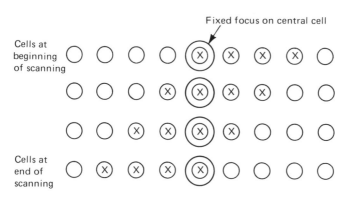

Figure 3.8
Scanning across the visual buffer. X indicates activity in cell.

attended to during scanning—namely, those that lie in the fixed region of central focus—remain the same.

Kosslyn maintains that the scanning process normally, though not always, operates as he supposes it does in the cited experiments.[33] He notes, for example, that "it seems easy to scan around the four walls of an imaged room, never 'bumping into an edge'."[34] This would not be possible, if scanning always involved moving the locus of attention across a fixed image pattern. For the pattern of activation in the buffer at any given time represents an object as seen from a given point of view, and points of view are restricted by the limited visual arc subtended by the eyes.

Why do subjects scan across their images bit by bit rather than simply letting them fade and replacing them with new ones whose parts have appropriately different positions, so to speak? One possible explanation is that moving an activation pattern already in the medium is easier. In other words, allowing an image to fade and then going back into storage to construct another appropriately different image may be more complicated (in terms of both the number and the complexity of the operations). If this is so, then, since effort in scanning increases with the extent of the transformations (and the number of iterations), there should arise a point at which the price paid to scan rather than to generate a new image is too high. It appears that there is indeed such a point.[35]

As to why scanning is done incrementally, one hypothesis is that such a process minimizes the noise introduced into the image by the transformation operation (i.e., the number of random neural events that interfere with and hence distort the image). Another hypothesis is that in the buffer there are hardwired connections only between those units that represent, when active, neighboring locations. If this is the case, and if scanning involves transferring activation from the unit attended to at the beginning to the one attended to at the end, then scanning will have to involve iteratively transferred activations.

Another important transformation process operating on mental images is the process of rotation. The experiments that Kosslyn and others have taken to establish the existence of this process were conducted originally by Roger Shepard and Nancy Metzler.[36] Subjects were shown 1600 pairs of block figures like those in figure 3.9 and asked whether they were congruent or not. It was found that, as the angular separation of the block figures in each pair increased, so, in linear proportion, did the length of time each subject typically needed to respond. When asked how they reached their answers, subjects reported imagining one figure rotated so as to superimpose on the

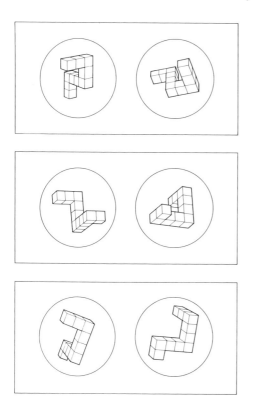

Figure 3.9
Reprinted, by permission, from R. N. Shepard and N. Metzler, "Mental Rotation of Three-Dimensional Figures," *Science* 171 (1971), pp. 701–703. © AAAS.

other. Conclusion: people can rotate mental images and at fixed speeds.

In a later experiment, Metzler took a group of the original subjects and presented them with a single figure.[37] She then asked them to image the figure (as seen) and to rotate the image in a clockwise direction. Based on calculations of the subjects' rotation speeds from the earlier experiment, she next presented rotated versions of the figure, the orientations of which should have matched that of the image. So, for subjects who rotated at 40 degrees per second, she "flashed" before them an 80-degree rotated figure after 2 seconds or a 160-degree rotated figure after 4 seconds, for example. Subjects were asked whether the imaged figure and the "flashed" one were congruent or not. The response times did not vary with the degree of rotation of the "flashed" figure, and they were uniformly short and positive. Metzler took this to show that she had matched the images at their intermediate orientations with the rotated figure.

The findings of Shepard and Metzler have been replicated in a number of other experiments. Their claim that mental images can be rotated is not to be taken entirely literally, of course. On their view, image rotation is a process that changes images in the same way percepts are changed during the perception of a rotating object. Thus, image rotation transforms images bit by bit so that they represent objects at gradually increasing orientations. This conception of image rotation is one that Kosslyn endorses, and it provides a straightforward explanation of Shepard and Metzler's experiments: Time increases linearly with increasing angular separation of the block figures because, with greater angular separations, more incremental transformations are needed in order to arrive at images that represent superimposed figures.

On the above view, there is a sense in which image rotation is an analogue process: it changes images in a way that is analogous to the way that percepts change during the perception of a rotating object. In a corresponding sense, image scanning is also an analogue process. It is sometimes said that image rotation is an analogue process in a stronger sense, namely, an analogue of physical rotation. If this means that image rotation is a process that makes images go through a series of ordered states that correspond one to one without exception with the states an external object would go through were it rotated, then image rotation must be continuous rather than incremental. This is not how Shepard and Metzler themselves think of image rotation (some of Shepard's own statements notwithstanding).[38] Nor does it fit Kosslyn's finding that the medium of imagery and perception has a grain. Nor finally is it supported over the incremental hypothesis by the results of the rotation experiments.

So far in this summary of the experimental data, I have said very little about the neuropsychological evidence. There is considerable neurological literature, however, concerning the loss of imagery following brain damage of one sort or another. Some of this literature suggests that the imagery system utilizes not only visual representations about the literal appearance of objects but also spatial representations about the layout of objects in space.[39] This presents no real difficulty for Kosslyn's theory, however, since the representations in long-term memory from which quasi-pictures are generated are taken to be both visual and spatial. In chapter 8, I shall address some significant neuropsychological data on image generation—data that are easily accommodated by Kosslyn's theory. In general, it appears that the patterns of deficits and continuing abilities that are found in patients with brain damage can be explained on the hypothesis that imagery is a system, the components of which are structures and processes conforming to Kosslyn's model.[40]

That completes my summary of the experimental data and its interpretation. I shall have more to say about both topics in chapters 4 and 5.

3.4   The Role of Quasi-Pictures in Cognitive Tasks

Why do we have mental images, conceived of as quasi-pictures, at all? What role do representations in this special format play? Kosslyn's answer is that quasi-pictures are useful for a number of different cognitive tasks.[41]

Consider the following questions: Which is larger, a mouse or a hamster? Does a bee have a dark head? Do frogs have lips or stubby tails? What shape are an elephant's ears? How many windows are there on the front of your house? Many people report using images to answer these questions. This alone proves nothing, of course—perhaps such reports are mistaken. But Kosslyn has conducted an extensive series of experiments showing that people indeed use images when they are required to respond to questions about parts or properties of objects that are, in Kosslyn's words, "poorly associated with the objects"—that is, parts or properties that people usually have not thought about in connection with the objects before, provided that such parts or properties are also not deducible from properties of the superordinate classes to which the objects belong (as is the case with the question, Does a bee run on gasoline?).

The fact that imagery is used in the above way can be explained given the following hypotheses: When we see a new object, we typically record certain facts about its structure by storing in memory a linguistic description of the object. But there are many facts we do not typically record in this manner, such as the shape of an elephant's ears. For facts pertaining to the object's appearance, we often store information in structures that are not lists of propositions or descriptions, information that we did not foresee needing to know when we initially saw the object. By generating a quasi-picture from such information and applying the appropriate inspection routines, we can easily answer questions about poorly associated properties or parts. Thus, just as it is much easier to see whether three cities lie on a straight line by looking at a map than by performing calculations on a list of descriptions of their longitudes and latitudes, so too it is often much easier to construct and examine a mental map or quasi-picture than it is to proceed in any other way (and often, of course, on Kosslyn's view, there will be no other way in which we could proceed, given the nonpropositional format of much of the information we have stored in long-term memory about the appearances of objects).

Another task for which imagery is useful is determining spatial relations among nonadjacent parts of objects. Suppose that I am asked whether the tips of a standing elephant's tusks are higher or lower than the top of its legs. This question is not difficult to answer if I am able to construct an internal representation of an elephant from which I can read off the positions of its various parts within a single viewer-centered reference frame, as I can, for example, by comparing the addresses of the appropriate activated cells making up a quasi-picture. But it is much more difficult, if the sole elephant representations I have available are ones that utilize "distributed" coordinate systems, that is, coordinate systems that only specify the positions, angles, and sizes of object parts relative to other parts of which they are immediate parts (e.g., the tusks relative to the face, the face relative to the head, the legs relative to the torso).[42] In these circumstances, I cannot simply compare the coordinates of the tips of the tusks to those of the top of the legs. I might add that a number of cognitive scientists believe that inner representations with distributed coordinate systems play an important role in shape recognition in visual perception. I shall have much more to say on these representations in chapter 4.

Images are also useful for solving certain abstract problems (e.g., Tom is wiser than Paul, James is less wise than Paul, who is wisest?). Solutions are achieved by translating the entities of the problems into imagined objects, applying the appropriate image transformations if any are needed (e.g., rotation), detecting the resulting spatial relations and properties, and translating back to the problem entities. So, in the case of Tom, Paul, and James, one can solve the problem very easily by imaging a dot for each person, and by placing the dots to the left or right of one another in an order corresponding to the men's relative wisdom. It is not surprising that imagery is useful here if images are quasi-pictures. Since a quasi-picture represents its objects as seen from a single point of view, it cannot help but depict their left/right relationships relative to that point of view.

In this chapter, I have tried to clarify the basic features of the picture theory of mental images within contemporary psychology and to summarize the experimental data that Kosslyn and others take to ground the view. In chapter 4, I turn to an alternative conception of imagery that also enjoys significant support among cognitive psychologists.

Chapter 4

Mental Images as Structural Descriptions

The view that mental images are quasi-pictorial representations has been hotly contested by some influential cognitive scientists. In this chapter, we shall examine the most widely accepted alternative account: that images are structural descriptions.

The composition of the chapter is as follows: In section 4.1, I explain what a structural description is and I discuss the charge that the descriptional view of images makes them epiphenomenal. In section 4.2, I explain how Zenon Pylyshyn, one notable descriptionalist, tries to account for the results of Kosslyn's experiments on imagery by means of the doctrine of task demands and tacit knowledge; I also summarize the experimental evidence that Pylyshyn takes to favor his approach. In section 4.3, I turn to the descriptional view elaborated by Geoffrey Hinton. This view, unlike Pylyshyn's, grants that there are special processes operating on mental images and a special format for imagistic representation. Finally, in section 4.4, I show how Hinton's approach arguably has no need of the doctrine of tacit knowledge, and I explain why Hinton believes that there is experimental data that strongly support his position.

4.1 Structural Descriptions and Epiphenomenalism

A structural description of an object is simply a complex linguistic representation whose basic nonlogical semantic parts represent object parts, properties, and spatial relationships. The explicit representation of properties and spatial relations is one key difference between structural descriptions and quasi-pictures. Consider, for example, the representation of relative distance relations in quasi-pictures. We saw earlier that this is achieved indirectly via the number of image parts: more parts, more distance. No explicit representation is possible here, since every part of a quasi-picture that represents anything represents an object part. In a structural description this is not the case, however. The fact that A is farther from B than from C can be represented by some such proposition as "$F(abc)$," where "F" is a symbol for the relation, and "a," "b," and "c" are symbols for the object parts. Since "F" is as much a part of "$F(abc)$" as "a," "b," and "c," there is in this proposition a representational part that does not represent an object part. I should add here that the relevant notion of part in the claim that structural descriptions have representational parts is not *necessarily* spatial. It has been held, for example, that among the parts of a structural description are the values of a "fetch" operation that takes the description as an argument.[1]

Another key difference between structural descriptions and quasi-pictures arises with respect to syntax. Structural descriptions have syntactic parts, the contents of which, together with their syntactic combinations, determine the overall representational content. In "$F(abc)$," for example, "F" belongs to a different syntactic category than "a," "b," and "c." Moreover, the content of "$F(abc)$" is different from the content of "$F(bac)$" even though the parts are the same. A quasi-picture has no syntactically distinguishable parts; and there is no syntactic order (so that two quasi-pictures that differ in what they represent must differ in what some of their parts represent).

The descriptional conception of imagery has been attacked on the grounds that it makes images epiphenomenal. As Kosslyn puts it:

> On this view . . . the image representations are merely "along for the ride", and themselves play no part in the cognitive processing. Whether or not we experience images, then, is beside the point. Images could be analogous to the lights flashing on the outside of a computer while it is adding. There is a systematic relation between the mental operations and the flashing lights, all right, but one could smash the bulbs and the computer would happily go adding along.[2]

There is much that is puzzling in this passage. In order to see whether there is anything to Kosslyn's criticism, let me begin by distinguishing two versions of the descriptionalist thesis. When a person has an image of an F—a tiger, say—there is an image that represents a tiger to the person. Call this image the "representational image." Many philosophers and nonphilosophers alike would say that when a person has an image of a tiger, there is a mental object upon which the image-experience is directed and which is given to the person in introspection. Call this image—the one that bears the phenomenal stripes (assuming for the moment that there are such items)—the "phenomenal image." Using this terminology, we may propose that one version of the descriptionalist thesis is (a) that the representational image is not identical with (nor does it constitute) the phenomenal image and (b) that the representational image is a structural description that underlies and gives rise to the phenomenal image. A second version of the thesis is that the representational image is a structural description that is identical with (or constitutes) the phenomenal image.

Returning now to Kosslyn, if we suppose that where he uses the term "image" he is thinking of phenomenal images and if we also suppose that he has in mind the first of the two descriptionalist theses I have distinguished, then we can understand everything in the quoted passage except the first sentence. And that sentence must surely be a misstatement; for no cognitive psychologist would posit representations that play no causal role in information processing. Perhaps what Kosslyn meant to say was that the phenomenal images—the images to which image representations give rise—are merely "along for the ride." Is the charge of epiphenomenalism justified against the first descriptional view? It seems to me that it is, if we follow psychologists' usage of the term "epiphenomenal," under which something counts as epiphenomenal so long as it plays no role in the brain's information processing. But, contra Kosslyn, it is important to realize that his experiments on scanning, overflow, and so on, do not demonstrate that phenomenal images are not epiphenomenal. What those experiments show, if they show anything, are certain facts about the structure of representational images. So there is no cogent argument here from the experimental data against the first view. Still, it cannot be denied that this version of descriptionalism is highly counterintuitive. On our ordinary way of thinking about imagery, we believe that phenomenal images are one and the same as (or are constituted by) representational images and relatedly that phenomenal images play a significant role in a variety of cognitive tasks. Suppose, for example, that I am asked to draw the two sides of a penny. My belief that this task requires me to use an image and that the image I experience plays an important role is virtually unshakable. This ordinary way of thinking is not absolutely sacred. But it does place a heavy burden of proof on the descriptionalist, if he or she adopts a position that runs counter to it.

The second version of the descriptionalist thesis I distinguished above is not counterintuitive in the same way. Furthermore, Kosslyn's comments in the quoted passage are clearly inapplicable: since phenomenal images are now representational images, they are obviously not epiphenomenal. Perhaps the claim that phenomenal images are structural descriptions will strike some philosophers as absurd. Does not introspection *demonstrate* that such a view is mistaken? No, it does not. It is, of course, true that when I image

something, I am introspectively aware *that* the object of my experience is a mental image, without being aware that it is a structural
description. But this no more shows that my image is not a description than my noticing *that* the person in front of me is Samantha,
without my noticing that she is the tallest person in the room, shows
that there are taller people present than Samantha. Nor does it help
to argue that images are not descriptions on the grounds that when
I introspect a mental image, I am not introspecting a description. In
this case, the argument is valid but it begs the question. In introspecting an image, I am certainly not aware of it *as* a description;
but if images are descriptions, then *what* I am aware of is one. The
general point, then, is that the format of imagistic representations—
the way in which they encode their content—need not be given in
introspection, even if such representations are themselves objects of
introspective awareness. All introspection shows, assuming that phenomenal images are representational, is that such images are representations phenomenally like those occurring in vision. I have
already made some remarks on this point in chapter 1. I shall return
to it in chapter 7, where I present my own view of the status of
phenomenal qualities in imagery.

So much for epiphenomenalism. Let us turn next to the specific
position of Zenon Pylyshyn.

4.2 Pylyshyn's Version of Descriptionalism

Zenon Pylyshyn maintains that mental images are structural descriptions no different in kind from the representations involved in other
areas of cognition.[3] In Pylyshyn's view, there is an inner language
within which mental representation, whatever its stripe, is confined.
This inner language is largely unconscious and is not itself a natural
public language, although it is translated into such a language when
we talk. According to Pylyshyn, Kosslyn's experiments on imagery
can be explained by reference to the task demands placed on subjects
by the experimenter's instructions together with facts the subjects
already know.[4] Consider, for example, the map-scanning experiment.
When subjects are told to scan across their images to an object they
are not presently focusing on, they interpret the instructions as requiring them to construct inner representations something like the
representations they would undergo were they actually scanning
across the map with their eyes. The subjects know that it takes longer
for their eyes to scan greater distances. So they set a mental clock
ticking for a length of time that permits them to mimic the response
they would give in the real scanning case.

It is important to realize that although this account is compatible with Kosslyn's claim that subjects are accessing serially image parts that represent adjacent, just noticeable map parts situated on a line connecting the appropriate figures, it does not presuppose that Kosslyn's claim is true. This is because the representations the subjects construct in response to the instructions may well not represent any just noticeable map parts; and even if some such parts are represented, not all of those lying on the appropriate line need be. Perhaps, for example, there is a sequence of representations like the following: "The hut is in the center of the field of view," "The hut is a little to the left and below the center of the field of view," "The hut is as far below and to the left of the center of the field of view as the lake is above and to the right," "The lake is in the center of the field of view." And perhaps there is also a symbolic representation of the distance on the map between the lake and the hut. On this conception of what is going on, for different distances scanned there may be no corresponding difference in the number of representations or parts thereof. So, Pylyshyn claims, the map-scanning experiment does not demonstrate that subjects are transforming a special quasi-pictorial image. And what is true in this one case is true, Pylyshyn thinks, for Kosslyn's other experiments on imagery. Subjects, in responding to the demands placed on them by the tasks they are set (demands built into the instructions), draw upon their (frequently tacit) knowledge of the world and their own visual systems. Thus, the data Kosslyn has collected give us no information about images as they really are.

There is a second view, similar to Pylyshyn's, according to which the imagery data are produced, not because of task demands implicit in the instructions, but because the subjects guess the predictions of the experiments and then use their guesses to control their responses.[5] This view provides the descriptionalist with respect to images with an alternative account of the experiments motivating pictorialism. Of course, it is also open to the descriptionalist to appeal to Pylyshyn's task demands account for some experiments and to the "demand characteristics" account for others.

There are a number of well-known difficulties with attempts to explain away the imagery data in the above ways. To begin with, it is simply false to assert that task demands are built into the instructions of every experiment. Although such demands clearly play a role in some experiments (e.g., Kosslyn's map-scanning experiment, in which subjects are told to move their focus from one part of an image to another), there are many experiments in which subjects are asked to answer questions without being given any instructions about how to use their images or indeed whether to use them at all. Recall, for example, the scanning experiment of Finke and Pinker or the rotation experiment of Shepard and Metzler. In the former case, subjects were not told to scan across the images they had formed, and in the latter, they were not told to form mental images at all. Of course, the demand characteristics account could still be appealed to for these and other such cases. But the results do not change even if the only data used are those obtained during debriefing after the experiments from subjects who have not guessed the correct hypotheses.[6] It is also interesting to note that when subjects are asked after the experiments to specify what they think is the correct hypothesis, they often get it wrong. For example, in the map-scanning experiment, several subjects claimed that they scanned more slowly across shorter (represented) distances.[7] This claim was at odds with their actual scanning times. I suppose it might still be claimed that subjects unconsciously knew the correct hypotheses, whatever they said to the experimenters. But this is a pretty desperate position, for which there is no evidence; and if the descriptionalist is reduced to adopting it, he or she is on very shaky ground.

A second, related difficulty for the demand approach to the imagery data concerns the claim that subjects draw upon their knowledge, often tacit, of visual perception and the physical world. The trouble here is straightforward enough: the claim is false in many cases. For one thing, there are a number of counterintuitive imagery phenomena that have been discovered in novel laboratory settings, such as the imagistic McCollough effect.[8] These phenomena are not found in everyday perception and are initially viewed with skepticism by many people. For another thing, there are some subtle differences between imagery and perception. For example, it has been found that when images are spontaneously generated, the apparent size of the imaged object is different from the typical perceived apparent size of the object.[9] This difference is inexplicable, if subjects simply construct their images by recalling the object sizes in typical instances of perception. It appears, then, that it cannot always be true that in imagery subjects draw upon their tacit knowledge of perception or the physical world.

The last point I want to make concerning task demands or demand characteristics is that even if it is true that people do sometimes draw upon their knowledge of perceptual situations when they image, the question remains why perceptual representations have the character and limits they do. Why, for example, do larger objects begin to "overflow" from the field of view at greater distances than smaller ones? Why is the perceptual field roughly circular? Why can't we see a four-dimensional cube? These questions deserve answers. Unfortunately, there is nothing in the demands approach that supplies them.

Pylyshyn has recently conceded that the appeal to task demands will not explain the results of all the scanning experiments. In particular, he now admits that Finke and Pinker's scanning experiment is not subject to the task demands criticism. Pylyshyn's present account of the results of this experiment can be brought out as follows.[10] To begin with, Pylyshyn hypothesizes that there is a preattentive mechanism in the visual system for indexing the locations of features within the visual field. This mechanism is very primitive: before the visual system can begin to recognize patterns or encode the relative locations of features within the visual field, it must first index or point to the relevant features. This pointing is accomplished, Pylyshyn maintains, without the visual system first identifying what feature is being pointed to.

Now, in Finke and Pinker's experiment, subjects were perceptually presented with a pattern of dots on a screen. The pattern was removed and an arrow was flashed before the subjects' eyes. Subjects were asked whether the arrow pointed to where a dot had been located. In those cases where the answer was yes, the time of response increased linearly with the distance from the tip of the arrow to the dot. What is going on here, according to Pylyshyn, is that the subjects' visual systems first index various places filled with dots. Conceptual "labels" are then associated with these places, thereby enabling the subjects to respond to the task, when the arrow is flashed on the screen, as they would were the dots still physically present.

Exactly how this is done is not clear from Pylyshyn's very brief discussion of the matter.[11] On one interpretation of his remarks, what the subjects do is to move the locus of their focused attention (without moving their eyes) from one place to another—just as they would were they really eye scanning across the scene from the tip of the arrow to a real dot. The result is that time increases linearly with distance in the imagery case just as in the perceptual case. On an alternative interpretation, Pylyshyn's view is that there really is no serial scanning in the experiment. Rather, the subjects compute the distances from the tip of the arrow to the places previously occupied by dots, and then they use their tacit knowledge of the fact that it takes longer for their eyes to scan greater distances, to time their responses so as to imitate those they would give in the real eye-scanning case.

On the former reading, Pylyshyn is now prepared to admit image scanning of precisely the sort that Kosslyn countenances. Thus, Pylyshyn is no longer entitled to claim that the scanning data provide us with no information about images, as they really are. On the contrary, he must now accept a key feature of Kosslyn's position. On the latter reading, Pylyshyn's present view is very much like his original one, since there remains a central appeal to tacit knowledge. This appeal, of course, is problematic in the ways I earlier indicated.

I come finally to the experimental data that Pylyshyn has adduced in support of the general view that mental images are structural descriptions. These data are basically of two sorts: data pertaining to cognitive penetrability and data pertaining to image indeterminacy. I begin with the former. In one experiment performed by Pylyshyn, subjects were shown two sets of figures like those in figure 4.1.[12] Subjects were told to rotate the figure on the left until its top coincided with the arrow in the right-hand figure and then to judge whether the latter figure was a subpart of the former. Pylyshyn found that the rate of rotation was affected by the goodness (in the Gestalt sense) of the right-hand figure. In those cases where the right-hand figure is a good subpart of the left-hand figure (as in part (a) of figure 4.1), the rotation rate was faster. Pylyshyn also discovered that the rotation rates for images of more complex figures are slower, and that with practice rotation rates typically become faster. The immediate conclusion Pylyshyn draws is that the rotation process is cognitively penetrable, that is, its operation is sensitive to the contents of a person's beliefs. And what is true here for rotation is true also for the scanning process, or so Pylyshyn maintains. For example, the rate of scanning can be affected by getting the scanner to imagine that a small black spot is moving across the image as scanning occurs: when the person thinks of the dot as very dense and heavy, the scanning rate is slower. Why does it matter whether image transformation processes are cognitively penetrable? Well, if the mode of operation of such processes can be influenced by people's beliefs and knowledge, then the processes cannot be basic, fixed parts of the cognitive architecture, as Kosslyn seems to suppose, and there is no longer any reason to assert that imagery involves operations different from those that manipulate the representations underlying knowledge in general.

Pylyshyn claims that facts about image indeterminacy also support the view that images are structural descriptions.[13] For example, when 4-year-old children are shown an inclined beaker containing a colored fluid and are later asked to draw what they saw, they usually draw the fluid level perpendicular to the sides of the beaker, as shown in

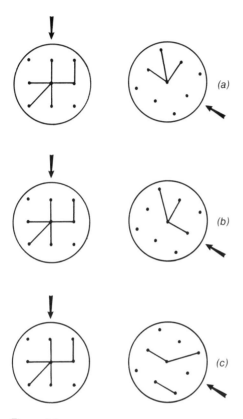

Figure 4.1
(a) "Yes" item; good subfigure. (b) "Yes" item; poor subfigure. (c) "No" item. Adapted, with permission, from Zenon Pylyshyn, "The Rate of 'Mental Rotation' of Images: A Test of a Holistic Analogue Hypothesis," *Memory and Cognition* 7 (1979), pp. 19–28. Reprinted by permission of Psychonomic Society, Inc.

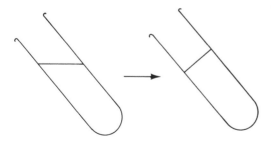

Figure 4.2
An inclined beaker containing fluid and the children's drawing of it.

figure 4.2. Similarly, when young children are shown a small object being positioned next to a container (e.g., a jug) and are then asked to duplicate the observed action, they typically put the object inside the container, as shown in figure 4.3.

On the assumption that images are descriptions, these errors are easily accounted for, according to Pylyshyn. In the tilted beaker case, the children construct an inner description out of the concepts they possess. Since they lack the concept "geocentric level," they cannot construct the same description as an adult. They therefore utilize a neighboring concept, typically "perpendicular," and they produce a description that does not quite match the observed situation. Thus, an error results in their drawings. The second case has a similar explanation. Here the children lack the concept "next to." When they originally are shown the object being placed next to the container, they see only that the object is in some proximate relation to the container. Thus, the inner description they generate as they view the action is conceptually less differentiated than that of an adult. In imitating the action, the children are guided by the earlier description, and they select an action of their own that is not only compatible with the description but also preferred to other compatible actions. It turns out that this action consists of placing the object inside the container.

Pylyshyn maintains that the pictorial view of images cannot explain these facts. If images are like inner pictures that simply reproduce "snapshots" taken in perception, then there will be no differences between the children's images in the above cases and those of adults. The errors the children produce will therefore be inexplicable.

Another phenomenon Pylyshyn takes to lend strong support to the descriptionalist position is the hugely superior visual memory that chess masters have for board positions (after only a few seconds'

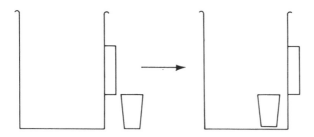

Figure 4.3
Young children place the cup inside the jug when asked to copy the experimenter's action of putting the cup next to the jug.

exposure) in comparison with mediocre chess players.[14] What is striking is that the difference between the two groups disappears when a random arrangement of chess pieces is presented instead of a real board position. If the masters construct inner pictures of the arrangements of pieces that they "view" when they reconstruct the arrangements, there is, so Pylyshyn claims, no reason for them to do much better with the true board positions. But if the images they form are really structural descriptions, then we should expect a striking difference in the two cases. For the chess masters have a rich internal vocabulary for real-life chess positions, a vocabulary that describes the positions in terms of various common constituent chess configurations and includes such concepts as attack, control, and defense as well as concepts pertaining to the configurations' geometrical patterns. This vocabulary enables the masters to construct very quickly representations that draw on their superior knowledge of standard chess positions and that are, as a result, descriptively much more powerful than those available to the weak chess players.

In a later chapter, I shall consider whether these arguments for descriptionalism are compelling. For the moment, I turn to an alternative version of the view that images are structural descriptions.

4.3   Hinton's View

Geoffrey Hinton has developed an interesting account of imagery that is much more explicit than Pylyshyn's on such matters as image generation and the need for a special format for information represented in images.[15] Like Pylyshyn, Hinton denies that there is a special medium, the cells of which represent, when active, small patches of object surface. Unlike Pylyshyn, Hinton asserts that imagery is essentially made up of viewer-centered information affixed to object-centered structural descriptions of objects' shapes. This needs a little explanation.

According to Hinton, when a person forms a mental image of a horse, say, he or she activates various components of a hierarchical description, stored in long-term memory, of a horse's shape. To say that the description is hierarchically structured is to say that it involves a number of different connected descriptions of entire (natural) horse parts, each with its own coordinate system centered on the relevant part, rather than a single description specifying the overall shape relative to a single coordinate system. Thus, there is a top-level description of the largest horse part (its torso), specified in terms of a coordinate system centered on the torso. In this description, there is also information about the locations, angles, and lengths of the other main parts of the horse (its head, tail, and legs). Next there are descriptions of each of these main parts. Each description has a coordinate system centered on the relevant part or on the largest part of that part (e.g., on the neck axis for the head part). Again there is information within each description of the locations, lengths, and angles of the parts that make up each main part. Each of these subordinate parts, in turn, has a further description centered on it that also contains information about still further subordinate parts, and so on.

One large class of shapes that have natural axes based on their elongation or symmetry are generalized cones (e.g., cylinders).[16] Since such shapes have well-defined axes, it is easy to define object-centered coordinate systems for them. In the above example, the shapes of the horse parts are taken to be generalized cones.[17] Hence, no difficulty arises in defining appropriate coordinate systems.

The basic idea, then, is that in generating a mental image of a horse, say, a person activates some subset of the set of representations constituting a hierarchical description of a horse's shape. This is not all that occurs, however, for mental images represent objects as seen from given points of view. So, further representations are constructed of the locations of the various horse parts relative to a reference frame centered on the viewer, and these representations are appended to the descriptions of the parts in the object-centered description. The computation is performed as follows: First, a viewer-centered location is chosen for some horse part (e.g., the torso). Next, further compatible viewer-centered locations are assigned to other horse parts using the initial location, together with some subset of the intrinsic object-centered locations represented in the hierarchical description. The overall view is shown in figure 4.4.

4.4   The Experimental Evidence for Hinton's View and the Issue of Tacit Knowledge

In Hinton's theory, there is no need to deny that there are incremental image transformation processes such as rotation and scanning. These processes are accomplished by operations performed on the viewer-centered coordinates in the representations appended to the object-centered hierarchically structured descriptions. Basically, what happens is that these coordinates are altered gradually in just the way that they would alter during perception of a rotating object or during eye scanning of a scene. Of course, if a mental rotation of an object occurs that alters the orientation of the object not only relative to the "viewer" but also relative to some background objects, then

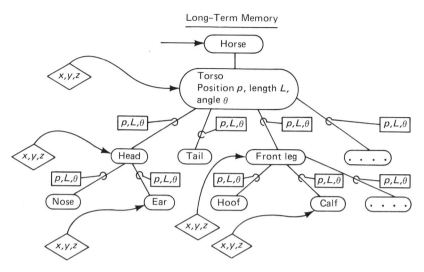

Figure 4.4
The basic components of Hinton's view. Generating a mental image of a horse consists in activating nodes in the hierarchical description in long-term memory, thereby bringing it to consciousness (indicated by the arrows), plus affixing global viewer-centered coordinates to the activated nodes (indicated by the 3-D coordinates in the diamond-shaped boxes).

more will have to change than merely the viewer-centered coordinates. There is no special difficulty here for Hinton's theory, however. For the representations of the intrinsic relative locations of the relevant objects in the scene can also be changed, and these changes can be as gradual as the ones in the viewer-centered case. It appears, then, that Hinton can explain the data on image rotation and scanning without positing a special quasi-pictorial medium for imagery and without availing himself of Pylyshyn's doctrine of tacit knowledge.

What of the data that Kosslyn cites in support of his claim that the imagery medium has a grain and is roughly circular in shape? Again, it appears that Hinton has the resources for an explanation that eschews tacit knowledge. In the former case, it can be claimed that the processes that are responsible for the assignment of viewer-centered coordinates to nodes in the hierarchical description actually only suffice to assign small ranges of values for the coordinates. Thus, when objects are imaged very small, nodes representing adjacent subordinate parts are assigned overlapping or even identical ranges of viewer-centered coordinates. The result is that blurring occurs, and it is necessary to "enlarge" the image in order to "see" the parts clearly. As for the data that Kosslyn takes to show that the grain of the imagery medium increases toward the periphery, Hinton can argue that a more economical explanation is achieved by postulating that larger ranges of viewer-centered coordinates are assigned to parts that are farther from the center of the "field of view." This occurs, it might be asserted, because imagery is like vision in many respects, and in vision processes assign viewer-centered coordinates to nodes in hierarchically structured descriptions in just this way.

A similar strategy can be used to explain the data allegedly supporting the thesis that the image medium is circular. In this case, we can suppose that when an object is imaged that fills the image field, the peripheral parts are assigned viewer-relative coordinates that place them equidistant from the center. This occurs, it might be held, because the coordinate-assigning processes function in imagery as they do in vision, and in vision they are constrained to operate in this manner. Of course, we are still left with the question, both here and above, of why the relevant processes operate as they do in *vision*. This question has a plausible answer, I believe. But it requires considerable stage setting, and it is best left until the general discussion of vision in chapter 5.

Before we look at the evidence Hinton presents against Kosslyn's view and in favor of his own, it is worth noting that the introduction of hierarchically structured descriptions in accounts of visual perception solves two significant problems pertaining to shape recognition.[18] The first of these may be illustrated as follows: Suppose that I identify an animal kneeling down in a circus ring, say, as a horse. If successful recognition involved getting an exact match between my visual representation of the horse's shape and a single (nondistributed) stored object-centered description of a typical horse's shape, then I could not make this identification. But with a stored hierarchically structured description matched to another such description generated from the visual input there is no difficulty. This is because the descriptions of the horse's front legs in terms of coordinate systems centered on the front thigh axes specify the arrangements of the front knees, calves, hooves, and so on, relative to those axes. And these descriptions do not vary with variations in the locations and angles of the leg parts relative to the horse's torso, however peculiar such variations may be (think, for example, of the possible variations in the positions of the hooves relative to the torso). It is assumed here that the descriptions centered on the thigh axes specify the locations, angles, and lengths of the leg parts not by assigning precise values but rather by means of ranges of values compatible with typical movements of those parts.[19] The second problem concerns the identification of an object as an *F* even though it is atypical in some physical respect or other, for example, identifying a crocodile with its tail removed. In this case, the hierarchical structure of the description limits the matching failure to a single component description. The matches elsewhere are unaffected and suffice to permit a correct identification.

Returning now to the case of imagery, one important difference between Hinton's structural description approach and the approach of pictorialists is that the basic representational units of the former represent cohesive object parts together with their locations, lengths, and orientations with respect to reference frames centered on overarching parts, whereas the latter represent small patches of object surface in a reference frame centered on the viewer. It is this difference that Hinton tries to exploit in favor of his descriptionalist view.[20] The suggestion is that reinterpreting ambiguous, complex, visual images should be much harder, if images are descriptional. Consider this example: Imagine two equilateral triangles of the same size, one upright and one inverted with its tip touching the middle of the base of the upright one. Now try to make out the parallelograms in this image. The diamond-shaped one in the middle is frequently found, but it is not at all easy for most people to find the other two. They have great difficulty in "visualizing" the two non-diamond-shaped parallelograms separating along a horizontal axis in the structure they have imaged. By contrast, it is very easy for them to "visualize" the two triangles separating along a vertical axis. Suppose now the original task is specified this way: Imagine two overlapping parallelograms that slant in opposite directions and have collinear ends. In this case, it is easy to "visualize" the parallelograms separating horizontally but hard to "visualize" two triangles moving apart vertically. Why is this? Hinton claims that the pictorialist has no good answer, since the image formed is composed of representational elements that are the same in both cases (each element corresponding to a tiny patch of object surface within a single reference frame).[21] The descriptionalist, however, has a straightforward explanation. When one forms an image of the structure in accordance with the first description, one activates an internal description, elements of which represent equilateral triangles and their spatial relationships to one another. Using this description, it is easy to visualize the triangles separating along a vertical axis. But it is not easy to "see" the two non-diamond-shaped parallelograms, since they cut across the two triangles and there is no explicit representation of them. When one forms an image of the structure in accordance with the second description, however, one does explicitly represent the two parallelograms. Hence, it is a simple matter to visualize their separating along a horizontal axis.

How, then, do mental images represent things? Are they quasi-pictures or structural descriptions? Or are they neither of these? What is the best account of image indeterminacy? How are the phenomenal aspects of images to be conceived? What is the physical basis of imagery? Are the contents of mental images really causally efficacious, as we ordinarily suppose? In the second half of this book, I present and defend a theory of imagery that attempts to answer all these questions.

Chapter 5

An Alternative to Quasi-Pictures and Structural Descriptions: Mental Images as Interpreted Symbol-Filled Arrays

In this chapter, I sketch a theory about how mental images represent things that shares features with the previous two views but is, I believe, superior to both of them. In section 5.1, I briefly present the basic elements of Marr and Nishihara's theory of visual perception. This theory is not without its problems, but it is widely considered to be the best theory of vision we have. I introduce it at this stage for three reasons. First, given the plentiful evidence that there are shared mechanisms and representations in imagery and vision, it is useful to have before us a plausible account of how vision works. Second, both pictorialism and descriptionalism take mental images to be significantly like certain representations (though not, of course, the same ones) that occur during vision on Marr and Nishihara's theory. Third, the account of imagery I favor draws upon central aspects of Marr's view.

In section 5.2, I elaborate what seems to me to be a serious difficulty for the pictorialist approach to images. In section 5.3, I raise some objections to the theory that images are structural descriptions. In section 5.4, I lay out the view of images as interpreted symbol-filled arrays. I show how this view incorporates aspects of the rejected theories, and I also bring out the links with Marr's account of vision. I maintain that the proposed view not only sidesteps the objections I make to pictorialism and descriptionalism but also accommodates a wide variety of data on imagery. I conclude the section by considering whether my position can satisfactorily accommodate both visual and spatial aspects of the imagery system; and I discuss a connectionist challenge to the general account of image generation I present.

5.1 Marr's Theory of Vision

The theory of vision developed by David Marr, together with his collaborator Keith Nishihara, contains several different parts.[1] I shall begin with Marr's account of the earliest visual processes and the construction of what he calls the "primal sketch." Since Marr's overall theory is highly complex, my discussion will of necessity be greatly simplified.

Light striking the retina varies in intensity. The initial idea in Marr's theory of the early visual processes is that sudden changes in intensity of light reaching the eye carry information about the physical surfaces of objects in the world, information that the visual system can extract and use to gain knowledge of those surfaces. Consider, for example, the case where two differently oriented smooth flat surfaces meet in an edge. Here the amount of light reflected by one surface will nearly always differ from the amount of light reflected by the other, and this difference will be signaled in the retinal image by a line of sudden changes of intensity. Matters are frequently not so simple, however. Some intensity changes are produced by changes in illumination and surface texture rather than by edges. Moreover, some edges do not generate sharp alterations in intensity. So it will do us little good to have visual systems that examine only sudden intensity changes. Evidently the processes that "look" at the retinal image must focus upon both sudden and gradual changes, and also determine which ones signal edges of objects. But how is this done?

Noise in the retinal image (i.e., irrelevant random perturbations in the light and the eye) can be diminished by operations that locally average intensity values. For example, one might average the values below by setting each value to the average of itself and the two values on either side of it.

5 5 4 5 6 4 6 8 7 9 8 8 9 8

Thus, the value 4, three integers in from the left, becomes $4\frac{2}{3}$, or rounding out to the nearest integer, 5. After averaging, then, the strip of values becomes

–5 5 5 5 6 7 8 8 8 8 8–

A better way of averaging values is to use operations that encompass a wider range of values but weight them so that the farther away a given value is, the less it contributes to the average. But however the averaging is done, the result is a smoothed array of intensity values, one that reduces intensity changes that have no significance.

After smoothing, the remaining intensity boundaries have to be found. Marr hypothesizes that the earliest visual processes find and represent intensity changes in the retinal image by detecting what he calls "zero-crossings."[2] To understand what this involves, consider figure 5.1 and suppose again that the numbers represent intensity values.

6	6	6	6	1	1	6	6	6	6
6	6	6	6	1	1	6	6	6	6
6	6	6	6	1	1	6	6	6	6
6	6	6	6	1	1	6	6	6	6
6	6	6	6	1	1	6	6	6	6

Figure 5.1

0	0	0	-5	0	5	0	0	0	-
0	0	0	-5	0	5	0	0	0	-
0	0	0	-5	0	5	0	0	0	-
0	0	0	-5	0	5	0	0	0	-
0	0	0	-5	0	5	0	0	0	-

Figure 5.2

One way of finding where the intensity changes in the horizontal direction is to consider horizontal pairs of values and to subtract the left-hand member from the right. Zero indicates no change in intensity, a positive number an increase, and a negative number a decrease. These changes can then be represented in a further array as shown in figure 5.2.

If there is a gradual gradient in intensity values in the original image rather than sudden sharp changes like those in the example above, there will be many more nonzero values in the constructed array and the most significant transitions will be marked by maxima and minima in these values. Such maxima and minima may be detected by subtracting the right-hand member from the left-hand member of adjacent horizontal pairs of values in the second array. This is shown in figure 5.3, where the result of the first subtraction is placed in the second column. In this array, maxima and minima in intensity values appear as zero-crossings, that is, transitions from positive or negative values. These zero-crossings can easily be detected by a process that is sensitive to changes in sign. Marr claims that our visual systems compute intensity changes in our retinal images by means of operators that are sensitive to zero-crossings *in*

–	0	0	5	–5	–5	5	0	0	–
–	0	0	5	–5	–5	5	0	0	–
–	0	0	5	–5	–5	5	0	0	–
–	0	0	5	–5	–5	5	0	0	–
–	0	0	5 ↑	–5	–5 ↑	5	0	0	–

zero–crossings

Figure 5.3

all orientations (and not just the horizontal direction as in the example).

Within Marr's theory, the operations of local averaging and finding zero-crossings are incorporated into one (the Mexican hat filter, so-called because graphically it looks like one), and the entire images are processed in parallel. Distinctions are drawn between sudden and gradual intensity changes by filters, or channels, of different sizes. Larger filters basically look at larger groups of intensity values. Such filters successfully pick up gradual changes extending over a large area (e.g., changes due to illumination). Small filters will detect highly localized intensity changes. All filters will register sharp and clearly separated intensity changes.

The next step, according to Marr, is for the results of the different filters to be compared and a representation constructed of the locations of edges and other surface details on the object or objects in the world that produced the intensity changes. Marr calls this representation the "primal sketch." It is, he maintains, a key element in subsequent visual processing. Marr takes proximate zero-crossings to indicate edge segments. Small sets of edge segments that enclose an area are called a "blob." Two close parallel segments are called a "bar." Some groups of zero-crossings are taken to indicate blobs and others bars. On Marr's view, the primal sketch is an array, the cells of which contain symbols that represent, at the associated (viewer-centered) locations, the presence of edges, bars, blobs, and corners.

This account of the early visual processes fits in well with our neurophysiological knowledge. In 1953, S. W. Kuffler demonstrated that the receptive fields of the retinal ganglion cells in the cat are circular, some having an excitatory center surrounded by an inhibitory region (on-center cells) and some having an inhibitory center with an excitatory surround (off-center cells).[3] The former cells fire if a small light is shined on their centers, whereas the latter are inhibited in these circumstances. Marr shows that a relatively simple combination of on-center and off-center cells will provide a satisfactory mechanism for detecting zero-crossings in just the way that his theory demands.[4] David Hubel and Torsten Wiesel's work also supports some of Marr's claims. They found that there are cells in the visual cortexes of cats and monkeys that are sensitive to oriented edge segments within their receptive fields.[5] They also found that these cells interact and are distributed in ways that are consistent with their performing local, parallel computations of the sort that Marr's theory requires for the construction of the primal sketch.[6]

The primal sketch is restricted to the representation of surface features in two dimensions. The next stage of processing, which brings in the third dimension, culminates in the construction of a representation that Marr calls the "$2\frac{1}{2}$-D sketch." At this stage, computations are performed on such things as the binocular disparity (relative difference in position) of objects in the images they cast on each retina, and the relative degree of movement of surface features of objects in sequential views of them.[7] From such computations, the depths and orientations (relative to the viewer) of small patches of physical surfaces are determined, and the question of whether an edge or a ridge is present is settled. Marr argues that the visual system, in performing these computations, utilizes a variety of physical facts about the world, facts that enable it to eliminate otherwise possible output values. The $2\frac{1}{2}$-D sketch gathers the output values into a single representational array, the cells of which are devoted to specific lines of sight relative to the viewer (with different cells devoted to different lines). Each cell contains symbols that indicate the depth and orientation of any tiny patch of surface lying on its associated line of sight, together with the presence of an edge or ridge, if there is one. What results, then, is a representation of the physical surfaces that can be seen from a particular vantage point when looking in a single direction. This is diagrammed in figure 5.4.

It is important to realize that the $2\frac{1}{2}$-D sketch does not itself represent the shapes of any objects visible to the viewer (e.g., whether they are cubes or spheres). Its concern is solely with patches of surface. Indeed, the $2\frac{1}{2}$-D sketch does not even segment the visible scene into objects at all. It is also important to realize that no top-down processing goes into the construction of the $2\frac{1}{2}$-D sketch. As Marr puts it, the purpose of early vision is to ". . . extract information about the visible surfaces directly, without particular regard to whether they happen to be part of a horse, or a man, or a tree."[8] Since the $2\frac{1}{2}$-D sketch changes as the viewpoint changes and since it

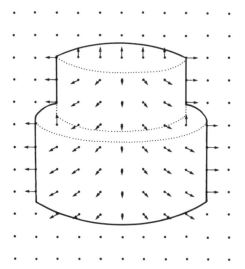

Figure 5.4
Here the arrows indicate orientation (the heavy dots are arrows pointing directly at the reader). The dotted line indicates positions where there is a ridge and the solid line positions where there is an edge. The distance of each patch of surface is not shown. From *Vision* by David Marr. Copyright © 1982 by W. H. Freeman and Co. Reprinted by permission.

does not explicitly represent object shapes, shape recognition of objects in the environment cannot simply be a matter of matching 2½-D sketches against stored (viewer-independent) shape representations. What is needed in the next stage of processing, then, is a procedure that generates from the 2½-D sketch a viewpoint-independent representation of the visible object's shape. Once such a representation is constructed from the visual input, it can be matched against stored, object-centered shape representations. Marr and Nishihara hypothesize that these representations, which they call "3-D model descriptions," are structural descriptions having a hierarchical decomposition. I noted in chapter 4 that the introduction of descriptions of this sort solves two significant problems for theories of shape recognition. There are also other advantages. For example, suppose I recognize the shape of a bear. With a hierarchically structured description formed from the input (i.e., a description that represents information about the shape of an object in terms of a hierarchy of descriptions of object parts, each with its own object-centered coordinate system), it is unnecessary for me to search blindly through all my stored shape representations until a match is found. Instead, I need only look initially at representations of the shapes of general classes, for example, four-legged creatures. Then, once a match is found here using information about the torso and limbs in the top level of the input description, a constraint has been placed on the shape representations to be checked at the next level down. This in turn places further constraints at still lower levels. Hence, the search for possible matches is restricted.[9]

According to Marr, information in the 3-D model description about object parts assumes that the shapes of those parts take the form of generalized cones. Given this assumption, it is not hard to define object-centered coordinate systems for each part. With respect to how the 3-D model descriptions are generated from the $2\frac{1}{2}$-D sketches, Marr regrettably has relatively little to say. Still, the overall view is extremely impressive and influential.

How do pictorialism and descriptionalism with respect to mental images relate to Marr's theory of three-dimensional shape recognition? Consider first descriptionalism. Both Pylyshyn and Hinton assert that images represent in the manner of structural descriptions. Although Pylyshyn offers no further account, Hinton claims that the relevant structural descriptions have a hierarchical decomposition very similar to that which Marr countenances in his 3-D model descriptions. Indeed, on Hinton's view, the only significant difference between mental images and 3-D model descriptions is that the former have additional descriptions appended to them of the locations of various object parts relative to the "viewer." Given this approach, it is not at all surprising that striking parallels have been discovered between imagery and vision.

Turning now to pictorialism, it is obvious that there are similarities between Kosslyn's quasi-pictures and Marr's $2\frac{1}{2}$-D sketches. Both are arrays, and both have parts that represent tiny patches of object surfaces. But there are also significant differences, the most notable of which is that the cells in $2\frac{1}{2}$-D sketches contain symbols representing such features as patch orientation and depth. These features are certainly not themselves object parts (unlike the surface patches). Thus, it is not the case that every part of a $2\frac{1}{2}$-D sketch that represents anything represents an object part. One of the crucial conditions for quasi-picturing is therefore not met. I shall return to this point in section 5.4 in the context of my own proposal.

5.2   A Problem for Pictorialist Approaches to Images

We have seen in earlier chapters a number of different objections that have been raised to the thesis that mental images are quasi-pictures. Although not all of these objections have been answered, I do not believe that any of them are compelling.[10] In this section, I want to raise a further objection that seems to me extremely damaging. It concerns the representation of the third dimension. How is this to be accomplished, if mental images are quasi-pictures in either of the two senses distinguished earlier? Do each of the cells or units in the visual buffer (the medium of imagery) represent, when active, tiny surface patches at different 3-D locations, or is the visual buffer arranged more like a 2-D snapshot that represents the third dimension with the help of perspective cues? In the latter case, the cells in the buffer will themselves only represent surface patches in two dimensions. The third dimension will get represented via processes that inspect the contents of the buffer and interpret depth cues much as we do when viewing a (real) photograph.

Perhaps someone might suggest that these questions can be side-stepped by denying that images do represent the third dimension. This conflicts with what introspection tells us, however. Moreover, there are experiments that support introspection here. Of the two alternatives distinguished above, the latter makes mental images picture-like in a more robust sense than the former. Unfortunately, it conflicts with the results of an experiment conducted by Steven Pinker.[11] In this experiment, subjects examined an open box, in which five toys were suspended at different heights, until they were able to form an accurate image of the display with their eyes closed. The subjects then scanned across their images by imagining a dot moving in a straight line between the imaged objects. It was found that scanning times increased linearly with increasing three-dimensional distance between the objects. This result strongly suggests that mental images cannot simply be 2-D "snapshots."

There is also good reason to reject the hypothesis that images are 3-D arrays. The difficulty here is not that the view commits its adherents to holding the absurd position that physical objects get replicated in imagery by interior 3-D models having the very same shapes; "distance" in a 3-D array is a matter of number of cells rather than physical distance, just as in a 2-D array. Rather, the problems are these. First, as Kosslyn has observed, the hypothesis is incompatible with data on image rotation.[12] This deserves a word or two of explanation.

Kosslyn claims that if the 3-D model is correct, then rotation of an image of an ordinary object should proceed at the same rate, whether the rotation is performed clockwise or counterclockwise (i.e., in two dimensions), or back to front (i.e., in three dimensions). This is because every patch of surface on the object (above a certain size) is represented in the 3-D array, including patches that are not visible from the given viewpoint. In back-to-front rotations, then, it is not necessary to retrieve information from long-term memory about locations not previously visible, as they become visible: all the information is already present. Since experiments reported by Kosslyn and performed by Shwartz show that for images of objects that are no longer physically present, the back-to-front rotation actually proceeds substantially more slowly,[13] Kosslyn rejects the 3-D model.[14]

A second problem for the 3-D model of images has been raised by Steven Pinker. His argument goes as follows:[15] Vision begins with two-dimensional retinal images. The three-dimensional structure of the visible situation is something that gets represented indirectly via processes that act on the two-dimensional projections on our retinas. Hence, perspective effects are found in vision. For example, objects farther away look smaller, a circular unmarked disk held at a suitable orientation looks elliptical. Effects of this sort are not found for the sense of touch. Whether an object is held close to the body or at arm's length, it does not feel smaller or larger. Nor does a circular disk feel elliptical at different orientations. The reason for this difference is straightforward: in touching things, we form representations of their three-dimensional structure without first forming two-dimensional projections. In this sense, touch is more direct than vision.

Now imagery is like vision and not touch as far as perspective effects are concerned. For example, when an object is imagined to recede from the imager, it looks smaller. Why should imagery be different from touch here? Surely, if images were 3-D arrays generated in a parallel fashion to those found in touch, then perspective effects would not be expected. There is, then, according to Pinker, reason to deny that images are such arrays.

This conclusion is bolstered, I suggest, by a related, more general observation. All participants in the imagery debate in psychology agree that imagery and vision share some representations and mechanisms. But there are no 3-D arrays of any sort in Marr's theory of vision, only 3-D model descriptions. On grounds of parsimony, then, 3-D arrays should be eschewed in theories of visual imagery (unless, of course, imagery data are discovered that can only be explained by appeal to such arrays or Marr's theory is shown to be badly misguided).

The overall conclusion I draw, then, is that representation of the third dimension cannot be satisfactorily handled by the view that images are quasi-pictures, at least if that view is understood in the ways proposed in chapter 3. So the pictorial approach, as it stands, should be rejected. I might add here that although Kosslyn has made some comments on the problem of depth representation in imagery,[16] there are other represented features about which he has, to my knowledge, had nothing to say and which deserve discussion. Suppose, for example, I form an image of a smooth red sphere against a yellow wall. My image represents the colors of the sphere and the wall, and the texture of the sphere surface. If every part of my image that represents anything represents a part of the object or objects imaged, as pictorialism in its earlier forms requires, then the colors and texture cannot be represented by image parts. In that case, how are they represented? Perhaps it will be denied that color and texture are represented in quasi-pictures at all and are instead represented elsewhere. But these qualities are certainly sometimes represented in images. Thus, images cannot be quasi-pictures. Alternatively, perhaps it will be said that color and texture are represented by *properties* of image parts, though not, of course, color and texture properties. This suggestion has the advantage of preserving a parallel of sorts with the representation of color and texture in real pictures.

5.3   Objections to the Theory That Images Are Structural Descriptions

One well-known and, in my view, compelling objection to Pylyshyn's version of descriptionalism is that it cannot satisfactorily explain away Kosslyn's experimental data on imagery by appeal to the doctrines of task demands and tacit knowledge. I raised this objection in chapter 4. I want now to press a further problem for Pylyshyn.

Pylyshyn, and other opponents of the view that mental images are like inner pictures, have devoted a good deal of energy to arguing that the view cannot accommodate vagueness or indeterminacy. In chapter 6, we shall take a close look at these arguments and the general question of how image indeterminacy is best handled. For the moment, I want to focus on what I take to be a plausible limitation on image indeterminacy. Suppose I have a single mental image of two objects, A and B, as seen from one and the same viewpoint V. Then, intuitively, my image must meet the following constraint: It must represent something about the direction of A to B in the context of V or at least their apparent direction. This is consistent with admitting that I might have two concurrent but independent images, one of A and one of B, without there being any representation of relative direction; for here there are two images, not one with a single viewpoint. Of course, even if I have a single image of A and B, I might simply fail to notice anything about the direction of the one object relative to the other. But this does not show that the *representational content* of the image is indeterminate in any pertinent respect.

For had I paid due attention to my image, I could not have failed to discover something about the relative direction, real or apparent, of the two objects—assuming that the cognitive systems involved in the inspection and categorization of spatial relations are operating normally.[17] In short, the relevant information is surely present in the image even though I may fail to extract it.

Advocates of the view that images are structural descriptions have often assumed that indeterminacy is no problem for their position, since descriptions frequently leave things unspecified (e.g., a description of a zebra may leave out the number of its stripes). What descriptionalists such as Pylyshyn seem to have failed to appreciate, however, is that limitations on representational indeterminacy in mental images create a potential difficulty for their approach.

The basic problem is this: It is just as easy to describe two objects, A and B, as seen from some given viewpoint, without saying anything about the real or apparent direction of A to B, relative to that viewpoint, as it is to describe a zebra without specifying the number of stripes. This fact presents a challenge to the thesis that mental images are structural descriptions. For my claim is that although a mental image of a tiger need not represent the number of tiger stripes, a single mental image of two objects must represent something about the direction, real or apparent, of the one to the other.

One move Pylyshyn might make here is to argue that in imagery people draw upon their knowledge of perceptual situations: we know that in normal vision we cannot have a single, integrated percept representing two objects, A and B, which leaves the apparent or real direction of A to B entirely unspecified (whether or not we cognitively extract this spatial information from the percept),[18] and we compel our visual mental images to conform to our perceptual experiences. This move is subject to the earlier general criticisms of the tacit knowledge approach to imagery. Here, I shall simply note that the response merely transfers the question to the perceptual case. What is it about the above perceptual representation of A and B that *necessitates* that there be any perceptual representation of the real or apparent direction of the one to the other?

Another move a descriptionalist might make is to claim that knowledge of the fact that in the physical world any two physical objects must stand in some relative direction or other places constraints on the representations available in imagery. Thus, when we construct mental images of pairs of objects, our knowledge of the physical world compels us to construct our images so that their representational contents are fixed in the manner I have supposed.

The obvious problem with this argument is that knowledge of the fact that in the physical world a perceptible object must have a color or a surface texture does *not* compel imagers having such knowledge to represent the color or surface texture of a perceptible object whenever they image it. Hence, the appeal to knowledge of the physical world will not explain away the stated constraint on representing direction in imagery.

What, then, can the descriptionalist say? In my view, the only really viable strategy in response to the above objection is for the descriptionalist to adopt the position, or something very like the position, of Geoffrey Hinton. On such an account, generating a single image of a scene containing two objects, A and B, is a matter of first appending a description of the viewer-centered location of some prominent part of A to the node for it in the hierarchically structured object-centered description of A (and likewise for B), and then appending further compatible viewer-centered descriptions to other object parts. This will be done via computations performed on the initial viewer-centered descriptions together with some subset of the representations of the intrinsic object-centered locations of A and B and their parts. However the details of these computations go, on the sort of approach Hinton takes, it is of the very essence of imagery that each imaged object and object part be assigned a viewer-centered location in the process of image generation. So, an image of A and B, as seen from some single viewpoint V, must indeed represent the direction of A to B in the context of V.

At this stage, before I raise any objections to Hinton's version of descriptionalism, it is convenient to return briefly to a claim I made in chapter 4 (but did not fully substantiate there) that Hinton's position has the resources to explain the data Kosslyn cites in support of his view that the image medium is roughly circular. My earlier proposal was (a) that the processes that assign viewer-centered coordinates in imagery are similar to those that operate in vision and (b) that in vision, when an object fills the field of view, its peripheral parts are assigned locations that place them roughly equidistant from the center. What I left unexplained was why condition (b) obtains. My suggestions now on behalf of Hinton are as follows: First, vision operates in more or less the manner that Marr maintains. Second, the $2\frac{1}{2}$-D sketch is roughly circular in the technical sense that Kosslyn attributes to the visual buffer. Third, in vision there are processes that assign viewer-centered coordinates to object parts by appending representations of them to 3-D model descriptions. To my knowledge, this is not a claim that Marr himself makes, but it is compatible with his view, and it does have the virtue of bringing together viewpoint-relative information and objective shape information into a single representation, as occurs, according to Hinton, in imagery. Finally, the processes that assign viewer-centered coordinates in vision to object parts do so by looking at the information about locations in the 2½-D sketch.

So far so good, then, for Hinton. However, trouble lies ahead. The first problem can be illustrated by reference to any question about object parts, the answer to which typically requires the use of an image. Consider the question, "Do frogs have lips?" People usually find it necessary to consult an image to answer this question. This simple fact is inexplicable on Hinton's theory. If, as Hinton claims, generating an image of a frog is a matter of affixing viewer-centered locational information to a hierarchically structured, object-centered description of a frog's shape, then there are two and only two possibilities: either there will be a node in this description for a frog's lips, in which case the addition of viewer-centered locational information and the construction of an image is entirely unnecessary— one need only look at the object-centered description to answer the question—or there will be no node for a frog's lips, in which case the same is true. Thus, Hinton cannot explain what Kosslyn takes (surely correctly) to be one of the primary uses of images, namely, answering questions about parts of objects that in Kosslyn's terminology are "poorly associated" with them.

I suppose it might be replied, on Hinton's behalf, that perhaps the only way, or the only easy way, the cognitive system can determine whether there is a node for a frog's lips is by generating the whole image and then "zooming in." But this really misses the point. As I noted above, on Hinton's theory, one cannot have a mental image unless one *both* activates a hierarchically structured description *and* appends to it viewer-centered locational coordinates. Thus, even if there is no simple or automatic way for one's cognitive system to gain access to given nodes in the hierarchically structured description without activating the whole description, nonetheless, once it *is* activated, sufficient information is already present to consciousness to permit one to answer the given question. Appending viewer-centered locational information to the activated nodes and thereby having a mental image of a frog is not *needed*.

There is another serious difficulty not unlike the one above. It concerns image scanning. Although Hinton admits that incremental image scanning sometimes occurs (via gradual changes in the viewer-centered coordinates), there appears to be no good explanation, on his theory, for why, in the absence of explicit instructions, anyone ever finds it *necessary* to scan. Take, for example, the scanning experiment performed by Finke and Pinker.[19] Recall that subjects in this experiment were shown a pattern of dots on a screen. The pattern was then removed and subjects formed a mental image of it against the screen. Subjects were asked whether there was an imagined dot toward which an arrow, subsequently flashed on the screen, pointed. The time of response increased with distance between the tip of the arrow and the dot. Thus, subjects chose to respond by scanning across their images. Why? On Hinton's view, there is no good answer. Since the mental images the subjects inspect involve descriptions of the pattern, in which the intrinsic locations of the component dots (plus arrow tip) are specified, image scanning seems completely otiose: all the subjects have to do is to examine the parts of their descriptions specifying the locations of the relevant dot and the arrow tip. I suppose it might be said that time of response would be expected to increase with increasing distance if, in each case, this examination involves activating the node in the description for the arrow tip and then transferring the activation along access paths through other nodes until the node for the relevant dot is reached. But it is pretty obvious that this proposal will not suffice to explain the *linear* increase in time of response with increasing distance.

The final objection I want to mention is raised by Kosslyn.[20] Kosslyn notes that there is no good reason, on Hinton's theory, for the rate of mental rotation of a subjectively large image to be any slower than the rate of rotation of a subjectively small image. This is because rotation, within Hinton's model, is accomplished by changing the appropriate orientation parameters, and it would obviously be ad hoc for Hinton to stipulate that such changes are controlled by changes in size parameters. But experiments have established that rotations of larger images are slower than rotations of smaller ones (assuming constant complexity). This result, incidentally, fits in well with Kosslyn's own view: if rotating an image involves shifting a pattern of activation in an array, with a larger pattern there will be more shifts to be performed as new cells are activated and so, as Kosslyn puts it, "lengthier processing at each iteration."[21]

The upshot, I believe, is that mental images are not structural descriptions. What, then, are they?

5.4   Imagistic Representation: My Own Proposal

The answer in two sentences is this: A mental image of an F (though no one F in particular) is a symbol-filled array to which a sentential interpretation having the content "This represents an F" is affixed. The array itself, which is very like Marr's 2½-D sketch, occurs in a fixed medium resembling Kosslyn's visual buffer, and is generated from information in long-term memory that consists in part of viewer-centered information about the visual appearances of Fs and in part of information about the spatial structure of Fs. This needs considerable unpacking and defense. Let me begin by making some comments on the medium of imagery.

Like Kosslyn, I believe that there is a medium shared by imagery and vision. This medium consists of a large number of cells, each of which may be either filled or empty. Filled cells contain vectors of symbols; empty cells contain no symbols. When a cell contains what I shall call an "O-symbol," it thereby represents the presence of a tiny patch of surface at a specific viewer-centered 2-D location; other symbols in cells represent color, intensity, texture, depth, orientation, presence of an edge, presence of a ridge. When a cell contains symbols for color and intensity but no O-symbol, it thereby represents the color and intensity at a specific viewer-centered location—a location that is not occupied by any patch of visible object surface. When a cell is empty, it thereby fails to represent anything.

Here is a simple example (very like the example of the cross diagram discussed in chapter 3) that ignores some of the above complications but illustrates the sort of thing I have in mind. Suppose that a group of men is shown the 3 × 3 matrix in figure 5.5, and each man is told to memorize whether some square is filled and, if it is, what color and intensity it has, with different squares being assigned to different men. Suppose also that each man is told to call out the color and brightness of his assigned square (assuming it is filled) when he hears his cell address and to remain silent otherwise. For example, in response to "(1,1)" the first man calls out, "Red, bright";

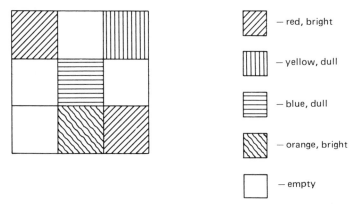

Figure 5.5

in response to "(1,2)" there is silence; in response to "(1,3)" the third man says, "Yellow, dull"; and so on. Each positive response, whatever its character, indicates that a square with a given location in the matrix is filled. The symbols within these responses represent the color and brightness of the associated filled square. They do not themselves represent its location. Had the colors and brightnesses of the filled squares in the matrix been different, some of the positive responses would have contained different words, but each would still have represented the presence of a filled square at the same location. In this sense, the responses are fixed.

So it is (given certain qualifications) with the medium of imagery. Each cell is dedicated to representing, when filled, the features I have mentioned at a specific 2-D location. As far as other characteristics of the medium are concerned, I maintain, like Kosslyn, that it is roughly circular in shape and that its grain increases toward the periphery. Of course, I do not intend these comments about shape and grain to be taken literally. They are to be understood now just as they were to be understood earlier in the context of my explanation of Kosslyn's position. My reasons for positing an imagery medium that is shared with vision, and attributing to it the above shape and variable grain, are empirical. I believe that these hypotheses explain very nicely the data Kosslyn and others have adduced in their defense and that no other hypotheses are successful.[22]

Finally, as I have already indicated, I suppose that cells in the medium are constrained to represent locations in two dimensions and not three. In my view, the third dimension (relative to the appropriate viewpoint) is represented by symbols within the cells, just as color and brightness were in the example involving the group of men. I take this view for two reasons. First, the evidence presented in section 5.2 is incompatible both with the thesis that the cells in the imagery medium represent the third dimension in the manner of a photograph (i.e., via perspective cues) and with the thesis that each cell is dedicated to the representation of the presence of a surface patch at a single viewpoint-relative 3-D location.[23] Yet in the scanning experiment referred to in section 5.2, scanning times increased linearly with increasing three-dimensional distance between the imaged objects. This fact is explicable on the hypothesis that depth is represented by symbols within the cells. Let me explain. In Pinker's experiment described in section 5.2, subjects imaged an open box in which five toys were suspended at varying heights. Scanning across the images required the subjects to focus on an imaginary dot and to imagine it moving in a straight line between the objects. If this process involved (a) assigning successive cells to the dot as it "moved" through space in two dimensions, and (b) for each cell representing the dot, simultaneously altering smoothly the symbol within it for depth, whenever there was any movement of the dot in the third dimension that was unaccompanied by any perceptible change in its 2-D location, then scanning times between objects would indeed increase with increasing three-dimensional distance.[24]

The three-dimensional scanning envisaged here will not be of the sort that Kosslyn countenances in his explanation of the map-scanning experiment. There is no translation of the whole image pattern across the visual buffer so that new parts come to fall under a fixed central region of attention.[25] Rather, scanning here requires focusing on a fixation point and then moving it across a stationary pattern. The processes that are responsible for assigning cells to the moving dot and symbols to its depth will evidently have to access information about the three-dimensional spatial structure of the entire scene. Hence, the imagery system must preserve in long-term memory appropriate spatial information. I shall return to this point a little later.

My second reason for supposing that depth information is represented by symbols within cells in the imagery medium is that the medium is shared with vision, and Marr's theory of vision, which I take to be the most promising theory we have, postulates that visual depth is represented in this manner within the 2½-D sketch. This brings me to my second claim about mental images, namely, that they are symbol-filled arrays very like Marr's 2½-D sketch.

We saw earlier that, according to Marr, the early visual processes culminate in the construction of a single representational array, each filled cell of which contains symbols representing the depth and orientation of the appropriate patch of surface, together with the presence of an edge or ridge, if there is one. In my view, if the appended interpretations are ignored, mental images are just like such arrays except that (a) they are generated from information in long-term memory, (b) they sometimes contain either fewer or more symbols within each filled cell, and (c) they sometimes have cells, the symbols in which represent the color and intensity of 2-D locations unoccupied by any surface.[26] The additional symbols referred to in (b), if any are present, represent color, intensity, and texture for the appropriate surface patch.[27] Such symbols may be missing, since images often leave color, intensity, and texture unspecified. And what is true here for these features is true upon occasion, it seems, for some of the other features too (e.g., presence of an edge or a ridge).

In calling images "arrays," I mean that they are patterns of filled cells in the imagery medium, patterns that are operated on by routines that identify cells representing adjacent surface patches (in two dimensions) as if they themselves were adjacent.[28] I do not mean that they are quasi-pictures in any of the senses distinguished earlier. On my view, mental images usually, if not always, contain within themselves symbols for surface features. Hence, it is not true that every part of a mental image that represents anything represents a part of the imaged object, as is required on the hypothesis that images are quasi-pictures.

It is also worth noting that the arrays *alone* are not images on my view. For there is no segmentation in the arrays of the represented scenes into ordinary objects, animate or inanimate, such as tables, horses, humans. The arrays, in and of themselves, merely represent surfaces and locations as seen from a particular viewpoint. Mental images result only via specific interpretations of the arrays. For example, an array representing a horse-like appearance becomes an image of a horse via the imager's interpreting it as representing a horse. I shall assume that it is correct to view thought generally as involving linguistic representations in some neural code, that is, representations having a combinatorial syntax and semantics.[29] Hence, I take the interpretation here to require the appending of an inner sentence with the content "This represents an *F*" to the array.

It may be wondered how the above approach can come to grips with the fact that an image of an elephant, say, evidently has parts representing natural elephant parts (e.g., ears, trunk, tusk) without introducing a much richer interpretation, parts of which are appended to the appropriate array parts. My reply has two parts. First, the introduction of an associated, highly complex description (e.g., one of the general sort countenanced by Hinton) is in danger of making the array itself otiose at least for some tasks. Suppose, for example, that you are asked how many windows there are on the front of your house. If you are like most people, you will resort to an image to answer this question. But if imaging here involves appending an elaborate structural description of your house to an appropriate array, then there seems to be no reason why the array should be inspected in order to discover the answer. It suffices simply to search through the activated description and count the number of nodes representing windows. The image, as a whole, isn't really necessary.

I suppose it might be replied that the appended description of the house may be incomplete and may not contain nodes for the less memorable windows, in which case inspection of the array will play an important role. The difficulty facing this reply is that if your image is accurate, then intuitively it will have parts representing all the windows on the front of your house. Thus, no account will have been offered of how those windows not represented in the description are represented in the image (i.e., array plus description).

Another possible reply is that the description will contain nodes for all the windows (assuming you have properly inspected the front of your house), but that searching through the associated description for all the window nodes will take more effort than inspecting the array. I grant that this is a possibility. However, there is a simpler alternative to the introduction of a rich associated description, which I shall now illustrate.

In the case of the image of an elephant, a given (proper) part of the image represents a given elephant part, I maintain, so long as it is true that *were* the imager to focus on that image part, he or she *would* consciously take it to represent the relevant elephant part. For example, a given portion, P, of my image of an elephant will represent its head, say, provided that it is true that were I to focus on P, I would interpret P in such a manner. Of course, this interpretation based on inspection requires the application of concepts, and one possible account here is that this proceeds via the construction of a structural shape description from P, which is then matched against a stored description of an elephant head. But the former description will be constructed only when P is inspected—it is not automatically associated with the array from the start, as it were, as part and parcel of my having an image of an elephant.

The importance of the overall interpretation in imagery cannot easily be underestimated.[30] On my approach, if two tokens of the same type of pattern of filled cells are interpreted differently, the two images will have different representational contents. Suppose, for example, that I tell you that I have a mental image of two hourglasses side by side as in figure 5.6. On another occasion, when working on a geometry problem, say, I have the same pattern in my head, but now I have an image of two overlapping parallelograms. The difference in the two cases is that in the latter, I append a sentence linking the pattern with parallelograms, whereas in the former, my sentence connects it with hourglasses (assuming interpretation is linguistic).

What of the following case? I form an image of a glass of water. My counterpart on Hilary Putnam's famous planet, Twin Earth, forms an image of a glass of twin-water, a substance that he calls "water" and that is colorless, tasteless, and odorless, but that is composed of XYZ rather than H_2O.[31] The salient difference here, as above, I suggest, is that my inner sentence contains a term repre-

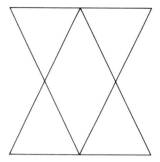

Figure 5.6

senting water, whereas his contains a term representing twin-water, an entirely different substance. How is this possible? Answer: in the same way that it is possible for his word "water" to have a different meaning from mine, namely, via different referential links with the environment.

The model of imagery I am proposing accommodates very easily another feature of imagistic representation that I have not yet addressed, to wit, the difference between there being one specific F of which one has an image, and having an image of an F though no one in particular. In the former case, the array is generated from information about the appearance and spatial structure of the given F, and the associated interpretation pertains to that particular F; in the latter case, the array is associated with an interpretation that concerns Fs generally.

Here is an example in which given Fs are imaged. Suppose that I am acquainted with two identical twins, Tim and Tom. Thinking of Tom one day, I form a mental image of him, as seen from the front, and thinking of Tim a little later, I do likewise. My images represent different people even though the patterns in my head are identical. The difference in image content derives from the fact that in the one case, the associated interpretation concerns Tom and is expressible in English as "This represents Tom," whereas in the other, it concerns Tim and is expressible as "This represents Tim."

There is also one other facet of imagery worth mentioning here that the model accommodates (with minor modifications). If I am asked to image something (e.g., Christ Church College, Oxford), I may do so by imaging a part of it (e.g., Tom Quad). This is possible, on the proposed view, if I *take* the pattern of filled cells I generate to represent not only Christ Church but also Tom Quad. Suppose now that I am unaware that Tom Quad is part of Christ Church. Having seen the quad and walked around it, later on I form an image of it. Here it seems to me reasonable to say that my image is also an image *of* Christ Church. But my interpretation concerns only a part of Christ Church, namely, Tom Quad. If this case is to be allowed, the account of de re imaging will have to be made slightly more liberal. Let us now grant that a person can have an image of a given object *O* *by* having an image of some part of *O*. More specifically, when an image represents *O*, as seen from viewpoint *V*, I maintain that the array must be generated in part from information about the appearance of the part of *O* directly visible from *V*,[32] and the associated interpretation must concern either *O* or any sufficiently large or significant part of *O* visible from *V*. The qualification "sufficiently large or significant" is introduced, since it seems counterintuitive to say, for example, that I can image Christ Church by imaging the tip of Mercury's extended finger (Mercury is a statue in the middle of Tom Quad) and interpreting it as such without reference to Christ Church. Mercury's fingertip is simply too small (and indeed insignificant) to count.

Before I turn to the final aspect of my proposal, which pertains to image generation (and associated issues concerning visual and spatial representations in imagery), I want to take up some of the empirical data Pylyshyn and Hinton cite against Kosslyn's pictorialism. I shall argue that these data present no difficulty for my own position. Consider first Pylyshyn's data on cognitive penetrability.[33]

In chapter 4 we saw that, according to Pylyshyn, the rotation rates for images vary with the complexity of the figures imaged and also their goodness in the Gestalt sense. We saw also that the rates of scanning can be made to vary by suitable changes in the scanner's beliefs. Pylyshyn infers from these claims that rotation and scanning cannot be primitive, fixed parts of the cognitive architecture, and that their operation is no different from that of processes manipulating cognitive representations generally.

Earlier in this section I commented on how I view image scanning. Let me begin my response to Pylyshyn by adding some remarks on rotation. I take image rotation to involve incrementally changing the pattern of filled cells in the imagery medium, while changing smoothly the symbols in the cells for depth (where this is necessary). As an image is rotated, then, the object it represents will smoothly change its represented orientation.[34] It follows, then, that image rotation without incremental change is impossible. In this sense, the rotation process is fixed. But it does not follow that the rate of rotation is also fixed. Perhaps *this* aspect of the process is variable in the ways Pylyshyn supposes. The evidence Pylyshyn adduces, however, does not establish this claim. As both Shepard[35] and Kosslyn[36] have observed, the rotation times for images of more complex figures may be longer because, with increased complexity, subjects perform their rotations piece by piece. Moreover, in Pylyshyn's experiment, in which subjects were told to mentally rotate a presented figure and then to judge whether it contained a second presented figure as a part, the overall response times may have been shorter when the second figure was a good part of the first (in the Gestalt sense) because the concluding comparison process was faster here.[37] Another possibility suggested by Kosslyn, which is also compatible with my proposal, is that as the image of the first figure is rotated, it degrades (all images degrade through time, according to Kosslyn).[38] With increasing degradation, the second figure will be more easily detectable as a part of the first, if it is a good part.

In any event, whether or not the rate of rotation can vary in the ways Pylyshyn claims,[39] the conclusion he draws to the effect that the operation of the process is no different from that of processes manipulating representations in cognition generally is clearly unwarranted. So long as image rotation has a fixed incremental character, as both Kosslyn and I maintain, it will remain specialized. And what is true here for rotation is true for scanning also. Hence, this argument for Pylyshyn's brand of descriptionalism is unpersuasive.

So much for cognitive penetrability. I come now to Hinton's data on reparsing complex images.[40] Recall that these data concern the great difficulty people have in reinterpreting complex images in ways that do not correspond to the descriptions they are initially given of the objects to be imaged. It should be obvious that there is no real problem here for the present account. Since the presented descriptions fix the interpretations people associate with the arrays they generate, inspection of the arrays is guided by the initial conceptualizations. Thus, it is hard to make out parts of the arrays that represent items not specified in the original descriptions. The problem is compounded further by the fact, noted above, that images decay with time of activation. This, I should add, is a feature of images that Kosslyn himself stresses in the present context. Kosslyn believes that images begin to fade as soon as they are generated. He also believes that generating an image in conformity with a complex description involves activating, one after another, groups of cells in the visual buffer that represent object parts specified in the description. It follows that any object part that cuts across parts specified in the description will be represented in the buffer via a group of cells, the members of which are at different "fade levels" (in virtue of their different times of activation). Hence, distinguishing such a group of cells in the whole pattern will be difficult. And this, in turn, means that reinterpreting the image in any way that requires focusing on or inspecting that group will also be difficult.

There is one body of data I have not yet addressed: that pertaining to image indeterminacy. The question of how to understand indeterminacy or vagueness in images has occupied philosophers, both historical and contemporary, as well as cognitive psychologists. Both the a priori arguments of philosophers and the empirical data deserve detailed discussion. I shall therefore postpone any further examination of indeterminacy in relationship to my own proposal on imagery until chapter 6, which is devoted exclusively to it.

I want finally to make some comments on image generation. I shall begin by considering a proposal made by Finke and Pinker.[41] Their view on images is closer to my own than any other I have seen in the literature. They too liken images to Marr's 2½-D sketch. But they do not (explicitly) maintain, as I do, that images are arrays to which certain interpretations are appended. According to Finke and Pinker, image generation is the inverse of the process that occurs in vision during the conversion of the 2½-D sketch into the 3-D model description. More precisely, they suggest that image generation is a process that takes information stored in long-term memory in an object-centered three-dimensional format, along with a specification of a viewpoint relative to the situation or object to be imaged, and computes from these an appropriate viewer-centered 2½-D sketch.

This is an interesting proposal. However, as it stands, it is incompatible with data gathered by Pinker alone, data that apparently have caused Pinker himself to give up the view he shared with Finke. In one set of experiments, Pinker told subjects that they would have to form an image of an object to be specified shortly, and he instructed them in advance to image it as seen from some particular viewing angle.[42] Pinker discovered that subjects could not generate an image of the appearance of a three-dimensional object, as seen from an arbitrary viewing angle, without first imaging the object in some standard orientation and then mentally rotating it to the desired orientation. This result is straightforwardly incompatible with the view that image generation is a process of the sort that Finke and Pinker earlier hypothesized.

How, then, is image generation to be understood? This is a large question about which I shall have more to say in chapters 6 and 8. What Pinker's data show, I think, is that the information in long-term memory from which images are constructed is partly viewer centered. Somewhat more specifically, I suggest, in light of those data, that generating an image of an F, though no one F in particular (an elephant, say), as seen from some viewpoint V, involves the following major components: (a) the construction of an appropriate pattern of filled cells, each of which without further interpretation represents merely that there is a patch of physical surface at a certain orientation and distance, relative to a standard viewpoint V', and having such-and-such surface features,[43] from information in long-term memory partly about the appearances of elephants relative to V'; (b) the association of the pattern with an interpretation, the content of which is that this (i.e., the array) represents an elephant; (c) if V is different from V', the performance of an appropriate rotation so that the pattern comes to represent an elephant as seen from V.

Of course, this proposal is merely a very crude, preliminary sketch. If, for example, the imaged object or scene is something the imager has never seen before, a cat standing on the back of a dog, say, then there will be no single stored representation of the relevant appearance. Rather, in this sort of case, the pattern of filled cells in the imagery medium is generated from separate pieces of information about the appearances of cats and dogs and the relationship of standing on. It is also worth observing that, even in the elephant case, there is evidence presented by Kosslyn that strongly supports the hypothesis that the initial construction of the pattern of filled cells is *not* performed all in one fell swoop, as it were, but instead proceeds bit by bit, utilizing parcels of information about the appearances of elephant parts.[44] Thus, information is also required by the image generation process about the spatial relations of parts of the imaged object: without such information there would be no directions for combining subpatterns of filled cells in the array into the correct overall pattern.

The claim that image generation draws on locational information as well as information about visual appearances of parts fits in well with what was urged earlier in connection with image scanning in three dimensions, namely, that the imagery system preserves information about the spatial layout of objects in long-term memory. Further evidence that the imagery system employs both representations about spatial relationships and representations about the visual appearances of parts is supplied by recent neuropsychological experiments, some of which are reviewed in chapter 8.[45] These experiments suggest that the two sorts of representations are handled separately in vision by two different perceptual systems, and that mental images are generated from these stored representations by means of two sorts of processes.

Before I close this chapter, I want to address an objection that might be raised to my proposal (and also to Pinker and Finke's) concerning image generation. It concerns whether it is plausible to suppose that information is stored in long-term memory in discrete data-structures or representations. Connectionists have argued that the phenomenon of graceful degradation of memory (i.e., smooth decrease in memory with increasing damage to the memory cortex) is difficult to accommodate on the classical conception, according to which memory is like a library or an office in which a large number of files are kept. On the connectionist view, memories aren't really stored at all. Rather, they are created over and over again in response to stimuli. We have *dispositions* to form certain representations given certain inputs, due to the weights of connections between nodes. This claim follows naturally enough from the general connectionist approach. In connectionist systems, information is actively represented as a pattern of activation in various nodes or units. When the information is not being used, there is no pattern of activation. Hence, information is not stored in any representations as such. Instead, it is tacitly present in the weights of connections.[46]

The claim that information is stored in long-term memory dispositionally seems very reasonable, at least in certain cases. Consider, for example, understanding a language. Obviously, we cannot store in discrete representations linguistic information about every sentence we can understand. When we understand a sentence (e.g., one we have not heard before), we do so because we have certain representation-forming dispositions that are activated by present stimuli.

Now if this approach to information stored in long-term memory applies to information from which mental images are generated, then we have a further reason to reject Pinker and Finke's claim that images are generated from object-centered three-dimensional descriptions, and we may also wonder whether the account I have sketched can be correct. Two facts should be noted, however, concerning my own proposal. First, as I pointed out above, all the available evidence on image generation strongly supports the view that it is a constructive process that draws upon separate parcels of information in long-term memory. Unless the dispositional approach to stored information is explained further in such a way that it can accommodate these distinct parcels, it will fail to satisfy this evidence. Second, my comments on image generation need *not* be taken to commit me to holding that, in the final analysis, the information in long-term memory from which images are generated is stored in discrete representations. Perhaps it is possible to make sense of the fact that image generation draws upon distinct parcels of information without holding that this information is encoded in discrete, stored representations. If so, then my talk of such representations may be viewed as a *façon de parler.*

I hope that I have now said enough to make my overall proposal reasonably clear and plausible, even though there are aspects that require fleshing out further. The approach I have taken draws heavily on the views of both pictorialists and descriptionalists, but it is not properly classifiable as falling into either camp. The problem with the theories I have rejected, as I see it, is not that they are completely wrong-headed but rather that they are only partly right. In some respects mental images are a little like pictures, but in others they are like descriptions. The truth about images, I suggest, is that they are a mixed breed.

Chapter 6
Image Indeterminacy

The phenomenon of image indeterminacy has occupied both philosophers and psychologists. In this chapter, I offer an account of image indeterminacy and I discuss various arguments, both empirical and a priori, that have been adduced on the topic. In section 6.1, I examine the major philosophical arguments from indeterminacy against the picture theory of mental images. I maintain that none of these arguments are successful and that, if anything, a priori considerations suggest that, as far as indeterminacy is concerned, mental images and pictures are actually very much alike. I also examine how my own view of images fares with respect to the philosophical arguments, and I give an account of the sources of image indeterminacy within that view. In section 6.2, I take up the empirical data presented by Zenon Pylyshyn. I show that Pylyshyn's arguments are effective against some possible versions of the picture theory but not against the version elaborated by Kosslyn or the symbol-filled array view I proposed in chapter 5.

6.1 Philosophical Arguments against the Picture Theory

Many philosophers have held that mental images are frequently indeterminate. There have been some notable exceptions, however. As we saw in chapter 1, Bishop Berkeley seems to believe that images can never be abstract or sketchy in any way.[1] Exactly why Berkeley takes this view is not entirely clear. It appears that he thinks of mental images as we would think of clear photographs. It also appears that, as far as Berkeley is concerned, introspection dictates such a position. It is interesting to note that most philosophers take precisely the opposite view. Indeed, the standard argument against a pictorial or photographic conception of images (and percepts) assumes, on the basis of what is "given" in introspection, that images (and percepts), unlike pictures or photographs, are sometimes less than fully determinate. For example, Daniel Dennett says the following:

Consider the Tiger and his Stripes. I can dream, imagine or see a striped tiger, but must the tiger I experience have a particular number of stripes? If seeing or imagining is having a mental image, then the image of the tiger *must*—obeying the rules of images in general—reveal a definite number of stripes showing, and one should be able to pin this down with such questions as 'more than ten?', 'less than twenty?'[2]

When Dennett speaks of the rules of images in general here, he is referring to the rules of pictorial representation. Since he holds that a mental image of a tiger can be indeterminate with respect to the issue of stripes, he concludes that mental images are not pictorial.

A somewhat similar argument is given by David Armstrong. He says:

The classic case is that of the speckled hen. I may be able to see that it has quite a number of speckles, but unable to see exactly how many it has. The hen has a definite number of speckles, but the perception is a perception of an indeterminate number of speckles. . . . the difficulty that this indeterminacy of perception creates for a theory of sensory items is that it seems to imply that the items are indeterminate in nature. The non-physical item that exists when we perceive the physical speckled hen will have to have an indeterminate number of speckles.[3]

In this passage, Armstrong is objecting to the view that visual perception involves the apprehension of a nonphysical sense-datum or percept on the grounds that such an item would have to be indeterminate. Unlike Berkeley, then, Armstrong thinks that *if* there are such things as percepts (and images) given in introspection, then some of them are indeterminate. Since there are no indeterminate objects (pictures included), according to Armstrong, there are no sense-data apprehended in perception.

Are mental images ever really indeterminate? It seems to me that before we can answer this question and draw any consequences for the picture theory, we need to get clearer on how the term "indeterminate" is being used here. Armstrong supposes that if a percept is of an indeterminate number of speckles, then it is itself intrinsically indeterminate. This seems to me much too hasty. The sense in which a percept is of an indeterminate number of speckles is this: there is no definite number N such that the percept represents N speckles. It certainly doesn't follow from this that the percept has an indefinite number of speckles actually on it. Indeed, how could it really have any speckles? After all, the percept, on the view Armstrong is opposing, is a nonphysical item.

One sense in which mental images are usually supposed indeterminate, then, is with respect to the representation of some visual properties. A mental image of a striped tiger, for example, need not represent that the tiger has fourteen stripes or ten stripes or indeed any definite number of stripes, or so at least it would seem. Another stronger sense in which mental images might be held to be indeterminate is with respect to some of their intrinsic, introspectively accessible properties (their phenomenal properties or qualia, as they are often called).[4] Here an image will be indeterminate if there are certain phenomenal properties such that there is no objective fact of the matter as to whether the image has them or not. To accept this form of indeterminacy is to give up the law of excluded middle. No such concession is required by the advocate of representational indeterminacy of images; for the claim that there is some visual property P such that an image I of an object O neither represents that O has P nor represents that O lacks P certainly does not entail either that the sentence "O has P or O doesn't have P" is not true or that there is any property such that it is indeterminate whether I has or lacks that property.

With these distinctions in hand, we can evaluate what I called earlier the standard argument against a pictorial view of images, namely, that pictures, unlike images, must be fully determinate. Suppose first that the argument is taken to concern representational indeterminacy. Then we may reconstruct the argument as follows:

(1) There are no visual properties such that pictures neither represent their presence nor represent their absence.

(2) There are visual properties such that mental images neither represent their presence nor represent their absence.

Therefore,

(3) Mental images are not pictures.

The obvious weak point with this argument is premise (1). Surely, there are often visual properties that are neither represented as present nor represented as absent in pictures. Take, for example, a black-and-white photograph of a fire engine: the fire engine is neither represented as being red nor represented as not being red. Alternatively, consider a picture of a man sitting behind a desk, as seen from the front. Whether the man is wearing shoes or a belt is simply not represented in the picture.[5]

Suppose now that the argument from indeterminacy is taken to concern intrinsic properties. Then it may be stated in this way:

(4) There are no intrinsic properties such that it is objectively indeterminate whether pictures possess them.

(5) This is not the case for mental images.

Therefore,

(6) Mental images are not pictures.

What are we to make of this argument? It seems to me that the most obvious weak point again is the first premise. Consider an impressionist painting of a striped tiger. In this case, the number of stripes actually on the painting may be objectively indeterminate. A second counterexample is provided by a picture, one of the colors of which is on the border between red and brown, say. Here it is neither definitely true that the relevant portion of the picture is red nor definitely true that it is not red.

A second objection to the argument is that (5) is not obviously true. Although, as the first version of the argument supposes, there are visual properties, the presence or absence of which is not represented in images (or so it seems natural to assume), it might be suggested that it is not at all clear whether there are intrinsic, introspectively accessible properties, the possession of which by images is objectively indeterminate. Still, if it is true that mental images have intrinsic phenomenal qualities—if, for example, it is ever true that images are phenomenally red, where there is not merely a matter of their sometimes representing real-world redness—then it seems quite plausible to suppose that there are images that are such that it is indeterminate whether they have some specific phenomenal quality, such as phenomenal redness. So the rejection of (5) naturally leads to the repudiation of imagistic phenomenal qualities generally. And many philosophers would deem this an unacceptable consequence. I shall have much more to say on this topic in chapter 7. My point now is merely that premise (4) is easier to attack.

The overall conclusion I draw is that the standard argument from indeterminacy is unsuccessful. There is a rather more sophisticated version of the argument that is not as easily dispatched, however. This version, which concerns representational indeterminacy, is due to Daniel Dennett.[6] It is now admitted that pictures *are* sometimes representationally indeterminate. But it is urged that such indeterminacy can arise in only two ways: either the picture is blurred, or the object it represents is represented from a viewpoint relative to which certain features or parts of the object are not visible. Thus, a blurred picture of a tiger may indeed leave open the number of stripes, and a picture of a man at a desk, as seen from the front, may fail to specify whether he is wearing a belt or shoes. The first premise of the revised argument, then, can be put as follows:

(7) Pictures cannot be representationally indeterminate with respect to the presence or absence of any visual property P, unless either they are (partially) blurred or indistinct, or the objects they represent are represented as seen from a viewpoint relative to which P is not visible.

By contrast, Dennett claims, mental images can be representationally indeterminate even without any blurring or obstruction to the relevant viewpoint. For example, a mental image of a champagne bottle may simply leave open whether it has "Moet et Chandon" or "Krug" or some other name on its label. So the second premise of the argument is:

(8) Mental images can be representationally indeterminate under circumstances other than those indicated for pictures in (7).

The conclusion, once again, is that mental images are not pictures.

This argument is, I think, superior to the earlier ones, but it is still badly flawed. As before, the problem, or at least the most obvious problem, concerns the first premise. As I noted above, a black-and-white photograph of a fire engine neither represents that the fire engine is red nor represents that it is not red. Similarly, a sketch of a champagne bottle may represent the writing on the label merely by means of a number of squiggles (not themselves part of any language). So the champagne maker may remain unspecified. A third example is provided by an outline drawing of an object. Here the picture will fail to specify all sorts of visual features. In none of these cases need there be any blurring or obstruction due to the viewpoint relative to which the depicted items are represented.

I know of no other philosophical arguments from indeterminacy that carry any weight against the picture theory. What the arguments I have discussed naturally suggest, contrary to their proponents' wishes, is that, as far as indeterminacy goes, mental images and pictures are very much alike. Admittedly, as we saw in chapter 2, descriptions are indeterminate in corresponding ways to those brought out above. So no advantage accrues to the picture theory yet. But in chapter 5 I maintained that there are limitations to image indeterminacy and that these limitations present difficulties for at least one version of descriptionalism. I want now to return to these limitations and to explain how they automatically emerge on Kosslyn's account of the picture theory of images.

It seems to me that there are boundaries on what may be left out in pictorial representation. For example, a picture of two objects, A and B, as seen from point of view V, must indicate something about the direction of A to B in the context of V or at least their apparent direction. Interestingly, what is true here for pictures seems true also for mental images.[7] This constraint on images was the one I focused on in chapter 5. It arises, on Kosslyn's theory, in the following way: Mental images, according to Kosslyn, are patterns of activation in a functional space. This functional space has a fixed number of units or parts that, when active, represent parts of the object or objects represented by the whole pattern of active units. Each active unit, in being active, represents the presence of an object part at a particular location in the field of view. Thus, there are no active units within the functional space that are reserved exclusively for the representation of directional relations among objects or object parts. Rather, the representation of such relations is fixed indirectly. For example, if object A is represented via the activity in one set of units and object B is simultaneously represented via the activity in another set of units, then an image I, composed of these active units, automatically represents directional relations obtaining between them.

This constraint on mental images, on Kosslyn's view, is also a constraint on other functional pictures. Consider, for example, the earlier functional picture of the cross shape in figure 3.1. Within that picture, each token of the term "filled," by being a response to a particular question, represents the presence of a filled square at one specific location in figure 3.1. So, for example, the fact that a given token of "filled" is produced in response to the question "Is square (3,2) filled?" represents that there is a filled square at row 3, column 2. Therefore, any two squares that are represented in the oral picture are automatically represented as bearing certain directional relations to one another.

What is true here for Kosslyn's functional pictures is true for my interpreted symbol-filled arrays. Since the cells in these arrays, when active (i.e., when filled with symbols), represent tiny patches of object surfaces at two-dimensional viewer-centered locations,[8] directional relations relative to a viewer in two dimensions will automatically be implicitly represented.[9] Therefore, the constraint stated above on the representation of direction in imagery presents no problem for my position. It should also be clear that the earlier arguments from indeterminacy against the picture theory cut no ice against my view. In the case of representational indeterminacy, either there will be cells in the array that lack their full complement of symbols so that one or more surface features (color, texture, etc.) are not represented, or there will be object parts, the presence or absence of which is not discernible on the basis of introspective attention to the array and what its parts represent. In the case of indeterminacy at the level of the possession of phenomenal properties, my proposal has nothing to say; for I shall argue in the next chapter that the view of images as interpreted symbol-filled arrays counts against the admission of such properties (conceived of as intrinsic, introspectively accessible properties in virtue of which images represent what they do).

6.2   Empirical Data

Let us begin our examination of the data Pylyshyn cites against the picture theory and for a descriptional approach with a look at the inclined beaker experiment.[10] We saw in chapter 4 that if 4-year-old children view an inclined beaker containing colored fluid and later are asked to draw it, they typically represent the fluid level as being 90 degrees to the sides of the beaker. Is this a problem for the picture theory? Consider first the perceptual representations the children form as they see the beaker in an inclined position. One possibility is that these representations are themselves representationally indeterminate with respect to the angle of the fluid level. This possibility is consistent with a pictorial view of percepts, since an appropriately blurred photograph of a beaker could easily fail to specify precise information about the fluid level. Similarly, a picture could be drawn in which both the fluid and the beaker are represented without anything further being represented about the relationship of the two except that the former is inside the latter, as in figure 6.1.

Figure 6.1

So, if percepts are like either blurred photographs or sketches (such as the one in figure 6.1), it may appear that Pylyshyn's experiment presents no problem. However, the pictorialist needs to say more here. Some explanation is needed of why the fluid level in particular is not clearly represented in the children's percepts—why, that is, there is blurring or other representational indeterminacy for *this* feature. I can think of no plausible explanation available to the pictorialist, if the children's percepts are conceived of on the model of blurred photographs mechanically produced by their training their eyes on the inclined beaker. So, it seems to me that any version of the picture theory that applies to percepts as well as to images, and which treats the former in this manner (however it treats the latter), is in trouble.

By contrast, if percepts are taken to be inner pictures that are drawn by their subjects, then there is no immediate difficulty.[11] For drawing requires the use of concepts, and it seems reasonable to hypothesize that the children lack the concept "geocentric level." Of course, if Marr's theory of early vision is correct, then there are at least some significant inner representations involved in the perceptual process that *cannot* be constructed in this manner. It also should be noted that some of the comments I make below are difficult to reconcile with a drawn picture approach to percepts.

Another possibility open to the pictorialist is to propose that the children's percepts, in themselves, are no different from those adults undergo when they view an inclined beaker containing fluid. There is, then, no representational indeterminacy, as far as the fluid level is concerned, in either the children's or the adults' percepts (assuming good lighting, etc.). Both sets of percepts are like clear photographs. Pylyshyn[12] seems to think that such a view *must* be wrong, and Ned Block, in a recent discussion of the inclined beaker experiment,[13] seems to agree with him.

I disagree with their assessment of the data here. A distinction needs to be drawn between the *percepts* the children undergo as they look at the beaker and the *mental images* the children later undergo for the purpose of drawing the beaker plus fluid on paper. What the errors in drawing directly threaten, I suggest, is the clear photographic view of images, not the clear photographic view of percepts.

It is worth noting here that young children have no difficulty in copying all the lines correctly when they are given a picture of the inclined beaker containing fluid and are told to trace the lines using tracing paper. If they can correctly discern the line in the picture for the fluid level, it seems hard to deny that when they perceive the beaker, the orientation of the fluid level is represented accurately in

their percepts (just as the clear photographic view of percepts supposes) and that they are *able* to notice it, whether or not they in fact
do so. This claim, I might add, is not incompatible with the admission
that the children lack the concept "geocentric level." Possession of
this concept is not needed to notice the orientation of the fluid level
relative to the beaker sides. After all, this orientation is the same as
the orientation of the sides of the beaker relative to the horizontal,
and, as all will agree, the children certainly notice that (see figure
6.2). To put the same point a little differently, the fact that the
children fail to grasp that changing the orientation of the beaker from
θ to ϕ, say, would change the orientation of the fluid level correspondingly does not support the hypothesis that they cannot
properly perceive the actual orientation of the fluid level as they look
at the beaker.

The conclusion I draw from the above discussion is that the clear
photographic model of percepts *is* a viable option with respect to the
data pertaining to the inclined beaker.[14] Turning now to my main
concern—namely, the *mental images* the children later generate in
order to draw what they saw—there are three immediate possibilities:
their images are like clear photographs, image generation here being
simply a matter of retrieving a stored percept of the beaker and fluid;
they are like blurred photographs, blurring being due to the decay
or fading of the percept during storage or else due to a defect in the
retrieval system; or they are like drawn pictures, constructed with
the assistance of processes that examine the stored percept. I shall
now argue that only the third of these possibilities is defensible.

The suggestion that the children's images are like blurred photographs faces precisely the same objection as the proposal that percepts are like blurred photographs: no plausible explanation is
available for why the fluid level rather than some other aspect or
part of the inclined beaker is blurred. The claim that their images are

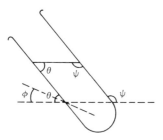

Figure 6.2

like clear photographs faces several objections. First, as Pylyshyn notes, there is the fact that the children draw the fluid level perpendicular to the sides. So a question arises as to why this and only this feature goes awry in their drawings, given that it is correctly represented in their images. Second, experimental evidence from children who are eidetic imagers is incompatible with the claim.[15] For example, when eidetic children are shown a picture of an elephant projected onto a surface, they can later image it very clearly on the same surface. But when they are asked to trace around their images, they produce stereotyped drawings of an elephant similar to those produced by other children of their age who have been asked to draw an elephant from a presented picture. By contrast, when they are asked to trace the elephant outline in the original picture using tracing paper, they do so without any significant distortions. This makes no sense, if images are simply retrieved percepts akin to clear photographs. On that hypothesis, both perceptual and image tracing should produce the same result.

A third objection is that the image generation process cannot simply be a matter of retrieving a stored photographic percept. This is shown by a number of experiments conducted by Kosslyn.[16] For example, it has been found that subjects require more time to form images of more detailed line drawings of animals. Likewise, when subjects are shown pictures of parts of a single animal on separate sheets of paper and are then asked to put them together mentally, thereby memorizing the appearance of the composite animal, the time it takes to form an image of the *whole* animal picture, upon later request, increases linearly with the number of pages earlier used to present it. These results demonstrate that images are generated from separate components rather than being simply retrieved all of a piece.

So, mental images cannot be either mechanically produced blurred copies of pictorial percepts (as, e.g., Locke supposed) or mechanically produced clear copies of such percepts (as, e.g., Berkeley held). But there remains the possibility that images are like drawn pictures constructed with the aid of concept-driven processes that inspect, decompose, and then reconstitute the original percept. This proposal can explain the drawings of Pylyshyn's children as follows: When the children view the inclined beaker, they pay little attention to the orientation of the fluid level, and so they fail to store any specific information about it. Instead, they store information about what the beaker itself looks like, together with *some* information about the fluid (e.g., its color) and the general information, couched in a linguistic or nonpictorial format, that the beaker contains the fluid.[16a] They call upon this information when later they draw inner pictures.

Since they lack any precise stored representation of the fluid level orientation, they represent it, in their mental pictures, in a way that matches standard cases with which they are familiar.[16b] Hence, they construct inner drawings of the beaker with the fluid level perpendicular to its sides. Contra Pylyshyn, then, the results of the inclined beaker experiment can be accounted for without adopting the view that images are inner descriptions.

The hypothesis that images are like drawn pictures also accommodates Kosslyn's data on image generation. Moreover, it fits well with the results of another of Kosslyn's experiments.[17] Here subjects were shown 3 × 6 arrays of letters (Xs in one case and Os in another). In each case, the array was removed, and the subjects were told to think of it as 3 rows of 6 or as 6 columns of 3. Finally, at the sound of a tone, subjects were told to form an image of the array, and to push a button when the image was complete. It was found that more time was required for image generation if the array had been conceptualized in terms of 6 columns rather than 3 rows.

This is again just what one would expect if images are like drawn pictures. For normally it takes a little longer to draw 6 columns of 3 Xs (or Os) than 3 rows of 6 (there are typically 5 hand movements from column to column in the former case and 2 hand movements from row to row in the latter). The conclusion Kosslyn himself urges on the basis of this experiment is that the way in which one conceptualizes what one sees affects how one stores and later regenerates the visual percept as an image. It is evident that this conclusion is compatible with the present proposal.

The drawn picture view of images finds strong support in the results of another experiment performed by Kosslyn.[18] Subjects were first told to observe grids containing block letters, like the one in figure 6.3. They were then presented with a grid that was empty

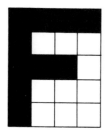

Figure 6.3
Reprinted, by permission, from S. M. Kosslyn, "Aspects of a Cognitive Neuroscience of Mental Imagery," *Science* 240 (1988), pp. 1621–1625. © AAAS.

(except for one or two X marks) together with a lowercase cue, and they were asked whether the corresponding uppercase block letter *would* occupy the cell(s) with the X mark(s). This is shown in figure 6.4. The positions of the X marks in the empty grid were varied for each of the letters. Now if images are constructed a part at a time (as they will be, if generating an image is like drawing a picture), then the response times should change with the positions of the X marks.[19] This was found to be the case. Furthermore, the response times varied in just the ways that would be predicted on the hypothesis that the image parts are constructed in the order in which the letters are usually drawn. For example, it was discovered that when a separate group of subjects were asked to *copy* the letters into empty grids, there was a highly consistent order to the positioning of the letter segments. This order was duplicated in the image evaluation task: more time was required to respond when the X mark (or one of the two X marks) occupied a cell on which a letter segment that was typically drawn later would fall.[19]

I come now to the second experiment Pylyshyn cites.[20] As we saw in chapter 4, this experiment required small children to view a beaker being placed beside a jug and then, a little later, to duplicate the action they had just seen. What the children actually did was to place the beaker *inside* the jug. As with the first experiment, the pictorialist can explain this result by supposing that the images the children form—assuming they form images at all—are like drawn pictures constructed, by processes that utilize available concepts, from distinct parcels of information themselves stored from parts of their earlier percepts.

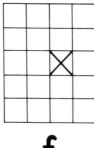

Figure 6.4
Reprinted, by permission, from S. M. Kosslyn, "Aspects of a Cognitive Neuroscience of Mental Imagery," *Science* 240 (1988), pp. 1621–1625.

When the children view the beaker being placed beside the jug, they fail to cognitively extract this specific information from their percepts, recognizing only that the beaker stands in some proximate relation to the jug. Hence, they store information about what the beaker looks like, information about what the jug looks like, and linguistic or nonpictorial information to the effect that the beaker is close to the jug. A little later, in responding to the instructions, they draw an inner mental picture of the beaker and the jug that represents the two as being close. On the hypothesis that this picture is drawn so as to represent also that the beaker is *inside* the jug (because, it may be supposed, the children think of the jug as a container, and they think of containers as standardly containing things that are close), the action they perform, upon picture inspection, is the one that would be expected.[20a]

The last piece of evidence Pylyshyn cites that I wish to discuss concerns the vastly superior memory chess masters have over duffers for real board positions (after only a very brief exposure).[21] This difference between the two groups vanishes in the case of random arrangements of chess pieces. It seems to me that this result presents no serious difficulty for the pictorialist who, like Kosslyn, thinks that the way in which one conceptualizes what one sees affects the way in which one decomposes one's percept and stores it. Since the chess masters have a hugely superior knowledge for standard board positions, they are able to construct a much richer description of what they see upon being shown a configuration of pieces from a real game. Having such descriptions at their disposal enables them to carve apart mentally each presented board position into a number of chunks, as it were, and to store information both about the appearance of each of these chunks and their connections (both geometrical and tactical) with one another. When they later generate mental images of the board positions, they construct their images piece by piece from this stored information rather as if they are drawing pictures. The reason, then, that the chess masters do better than the mediocre players only in the case of real board positions is that it is only in this case that there is a significant difference in the stored information from which the mental pictures are constructed, a difference that is traceable to their superior knowledge of chess and their richer conceptualizations of actual positions.

I conclude that Pylyshyn's data are powerless against the sort of pictorial view of images advocated by Kosslyn. So long as images are like drawn pictures, constructed from a combination of pieces of stored information, there is no problem whatsoever in explaining the results of the above experiments.

In chapter 5 I laid out and defended a view of mental images as interpreted symbol-filled arrays. I noted that image generation is best taken to be a constructive process of the general sort that Kosslyn describes. Thus, my defense of Kosslyn's version of the picture theory against Pylyshyn's criticisms applies mutatis mutandis to my own position.

The overall conclusion I draw is that a serious error has been made by those philosophers and cognitive scientists who have supposed that the phenomenon of image indeterminacy can only be explained adequately by theories that take images to represent in the manner of descriptions. Image indeterminacy is a problem for some unsophisticated competitors to descriptionalism, but for others, such as my own and Kosslyn's, it is a natural consequence.

Chapter 7

The Phenomenal Aspects of Mental Images

Many philosophers take it to be evident that mental images and visual percepts have, over and above their representational contents, intrinsic, introspectively accessible properties in virtue of which they have those contents. Such properties, which are held to ground the subjective character or phenomenal "feel" of the images and percepts, I shall call "visual qualia." Many an argument there has been about whether qualia, visual and otherwise, can be accommodated within a physicalist view of the mental, or whether they are special, irreducible properties. I have come to think that at least as far as imagery and vision are concerned, these arguments are badly misguided. I now believe that there are no visual qualia.[1] Therefore, the question of whether they are physical or irreducible simply does not arise.

This position will undoubtedly strike those (including my erstwhile self)[2] who have engaged in debate about the nature of qualia as puzzling indeed. Isn't it just obvious from introspection that there are visual qualia? Surely the only real question, many will say, concerns the *status* of such qualia. Challenges to their existence are no more worthy of serious consideration than challenges to the existence of tables and chairs. In what follows, I shall try to show not only that no good reasons have been adduced for believing in visual qualia but also that, upon proper reflection, the most natural view is that there are none.

The chapter is divided into three sections. In section 7.1, I say some more about what sorts of properties visual qualia are supposed to be, and what it is I am committed to in denying their existence. In section 7.2, I discuss a variety of arguments and examples that purport to show that there are visual qualia. Finally, in section 7.3, I make some brief comments on the overall significance of my attempt to eliminate visual qualia.

7.1   What Are Visual Qualia?

Consider a painting of a dalmation. Viewers of the painting can apprehend not only its content (i.e., its representing a dalmation) but also the colors, shapes, and spatial relations obtaining among blobs of paint by virtue of which it has that content. As we have seen in earlier chapters, it has often been supposed that being aware or conscious of a mental image or a visual percept is like viewing an inner picture. For example, on this conception, if I form a mental image of a dalmation, I am subject to a mental picture-like representation of a dalmation, introspection of which reveals to me both its content and its intrinsic, nonintentional features by virtue of which it has that content. These intrinsic, nonintentional features are not literally colors and shapes of parts of my mental quasi-picture, as in the case of a real picture; for it would obviously be absurd to suppose that a dog-shaped part of my brain is white with black spots when I image a dalmation, and it is surely no less absurd to suppose the same of my soul. Therefore, whether images and visual percepts are physical or not, even on a pictorial conception, their introspectible, intrinsic properties are not colors and shapes.

Anyone who believes that there are visual qualia must at least believe that images and visual percepts are like pictures to the extent that they have intrinsic, nonintentional features that are accessible to introspection and by virtue of which they represent what they do.[3] In denying that mental images and visual percepts have qualia, I am denying that there are any intrinsic, nonintentional features of which the subjects of the images and percepts can be aware, and by virtue of which these objects have their contents. This is not to say, of course, that the contents are not themselves introspectible. Nor is it to say that visual percepts and images do not have intrinsic, nonintentional features. If, as is widely believed, such objects are neural items,[4] they will certainly have intrinsic physicochemical properties.

The rejection of visual qualia is *not* tantamount to a rejection of the view that there is nothing it is like for the subjects of visual experiences.[5] On the contrary, I accept that images and visual percepts have subjective aspects—indeed, aspects that are common to both—and I maintain that what it is like to have a visual experience (what I earlier called the "phenomenal feel" of the experience) is determined by aspects of its representational content.[6] Hence, I maintain that any two visual experiences that are alike in all their intentional properties are alike in their subjective characters. To refute my position, it suffices to specify a clear counterexample to this generalization. I know of no such counterexamples. In section 7.2, I shall consider a variety of putative counterexamples together with a number of other objections.

7.2 Arguments for Visual Qualia Evaluated

7.2.1 The Argument from Introspection

Forming a mental image earlier today of how the Pacific Ocean looked to me a couple of summers ago as I stood on the beach in Santa Barbara, I found myself momentarily transfixed by the intense blue of the ocean, as it was given to me in my image. Was I not here delighting in the phenomenal aspects of my imagistic experience? And if I was, doesn't this show that there are visual qualia?

I am not convinced. It seems to me that what I found so pleasing in the above instance—what I was focusing on, as it were—were a certain shade and intensity of the color blue. I imaged blue as a property of the ocean, not as a property of my experience. My image itself wasn't blue. Rather, it *represented* the ocean as blue. What I was really delighting in, then, were specific aspects of the content of my imagistic experience. It was the content, not anything else, that was immediately accessible to my consciousness and that had aspects I found so pleasing.[7] This point, I might note, seems to be the sort of thing G. E. Moore had in mind when he remarked that the visual sensation of blue is diaphanous.[8] When one tries to focus on it in introspection, one cannot help but see right through it so that what one actually ends up attending to is the real color blue.

There is another rather different way in which a straightforward appeal to introspection might be made on behalf of visual qualia. The visual experience I had that day in Santa Barbara, as I stood viewing the sea, was, to my consciousness, very similar to a color photograph I might have taken of the same scene. My experience, then, was a picture-like representation of the sea, and my awareness of it was something like my viewing a picture. Since, as I noted in section 7.1, pictures evidently have accessible intrinsic qualities by virtue of which they represent the world, so too, by analogy, do visual experiences.

The most obvious problem with this appeal is that it is not at all clear that my visual experience, while viewing the ocean, was *really* similar to a color photograph of the ocean. The only undeniable similarity here is between my experience and the experience I would have undergone had I viewed an appropriate photograph.[9] The fact that these experiences are similar shows nothing about the way in which their contents are encoded. What I deny, then, is that the *format* of visual representations—the way in which they encode their contents—is given in introspection. What introspection reveals are simply aspects of the contents themselves.

My second objection is simply that even if visual experiences are, in an important sense, picture-like, it evidently does not follow that they have qualia. One could hold, for example, that visual experiences have intrinsic qualities by virtue of which they represent, while denying that these qualities are introspectively accessible.[10] Such a position still permits the possibility that visual experiences are picture-like, for example, with respect to the representation of spatial relations.[11] But it leaves no room for visual qualia.

7.2.2   The Argument from Hallucination

Suppose that Paul hallucinates a pink square object. Then there is something that Paul hallucinates. But what Paul hallucinates is not a real pink square physical object—after all, Paul is hallucinating, not seeing. Therefore, what Paul hallucinates must be a mental object, an idea or an appearance. Now mental objects are not literally colored, nor do they literally have shape. So the terms "pink" and "square" as applied to what Paul hallucinates must pick out special properties of which Paul is directly aware. These properties are qualia. Since seeing can be indistinguishable from hallucinating, visual experiences generally relate their subjects to mental objects, the intrinsic, introspectible properties of which are responsible for the subjective character of the experiences.

I shall not here comment on all that is wrong with this argument. When Paul hallucinates in the above case, he has an experience *of* a pink square object. This experience has content—it represents a pink square object. *There is,* then, a definite content to Paul's hallucinatory experience. But there is no object, mental or otherwise, that Paul hallucinates. Furthermore, the fact that Paul's experience has a certain content no more requires that there really be a pink square object than a picture's representing a three-headed monster, say, requires that there really be any monsters.

Consider the following parallel. Paul wants a blue emerald to give to his wife. There are no blue emeralds. It does not follow that Paul wants the idea of a blue emerald to give to his wife. That he already has. What he wants is that his wife be given a blue emerald (by him). His desire, then, is the desire it is in virtue of its having a specific content. When Paul reflects upon or introspects his desire, what he is aware of is this content rather than any peculiar qualities of a special mental particular upon which his desire is directed. Likewise, when Paul hallucinates a pink square, what he introspects, I maintain, is the content of his hallucinatory experience. This, it seems to me, is the commonsense view. The idea that the terms "pink" and "square" in the context "Paul hallucinates a pink square" stand for special, phenomenal qualities of which Paul is aware, and hence have entirely different meanings from those they have in, say, "The piece of glass is pink and square" is, on the face of it, very strange indeed. The argument from hallucination does nothing to make this idea palatable.

7.2.3 Visual Qualia without Representational Content?
Here is a related argument. Suppose you look at a bright light and turn away. You have an afterimage that is red and round, say. In this case, you are subject to a visual experience, but your experience has no representational content. What it is like for you, then, cannot be determined by aspects of the content of your experience. Rather, it must be due to visual qualia.

It seems to me no more plausible to take the terms "red" and "round," as they apply to an afterimage, as denoting intrinsic qualities of the image than it is to take the terms "loud" and "high-pitched," as they are employed in connection with the graphical representations of sounds, as denoting intrinsic qualities of oscilloscope readings. As we saw earlier, in this usage, what the terms really abbreviate are "represents loud" and "represents high-pitched" respectively. Analogously, it seems to me that what the terms "red" and "round" signify, in application to an afterimage, are representational properties of the afterimage experience. One who has a red, round afterimage is subject to an experience produced by looking at a bright light, the content of which is that something—typically a region of space—is red and round. There is, then, I claim, a definite content to the imagistic experience after all.

7.2.4 What It Is That Shoemaker Likes
In a forthcoming article, Sydney Shoemaker presents an interesting argument for the existence of gustatory qualia.[12] Although my concern is with mental images and visual percepts, I shall consider Shoemaker's argument since it applies mutatis mutandis to the visual case.

Shoemaker tells us that he likes the taste of Cabernet Sauvignon wine. This, however, is not all that he likes when he sips the wine. For the taste is some chemical property of the wine—some combination of esters, acids, and oils—and this chemical property could be detected visually with suitable laboratory equipment. In *these* circumstances using his visual sense, Shoemaker opines, he wouldn't like the taste. What, then, is it about the taste that he really likes? Well, perhaps it is the fact that he has a gustatory experience *of* that taste—that is, an experience in a certain sense-modality that represents the relevant chemical property. Shoemaker concedes that he does like having such experiences and that his liking them is crucial to his liking the taste. But what he likes about them, he insists, is neither that they have a certain content (this, he thinks, is established by the visual case above in which he has visual experiences with the same content) nor that they are produced by certain sense-organs. Rather, according to Shoemaker, what it is that he likes about those experiences is what it is like to have them, in other words, he claims, their qualia.

One way of attacking the above argument is to try to show that it requires an illegitimate substitution of terms within an intentional context. Suppose that I am drinking Cabernet Sauvignon and that I react in the same way as Shoemaker. I might state my satisfaction as follows:

> (1) What I like about these experiences is that they represent this taste.

If (1) is taken to assert that what I like about certain experiences and a certain taste is that the former represent the latter, then Shoemaker is justified in rejecting (1) for his own case on the grounds that he finds the relevant taste unappealing when presented visually.[13] (1), however, may also be taken to be referentially opaque with respect to the occurrence of "this taste." And if it is so taken, then Shoemaker's appeal to the visual unattractiveness of the taste is irrelevant. That such an interpretation of (1) is possible is evidenced by examples such as the following: Oedipus, after having decided to marry his mother without knowing who she was, might have said truly

> (2) What I like about my forthcoming marriage is that it will unite me with this woman.

Clearly, (2) would be transformed into a falsehood by the substitution of "my mother" for "this woman."

Shoemaker concedes that this reply to his argument is a reasonable one. Nonetheless, a question now arises about how (1) is to be understood under a referentially opaque reading of "this taste." For, as Shoemaker certainly realizes,[14] if qualia are to be avoided, (1) had better not be taken to assert that what is liked about the relevant gustatory experiences is that they represent the taste of Cabernet Sauvignon via their having certain qualia.

How, then, is (1) to be understood? This question is best answered in the context of my second criticism of Shoemaker's argument, which is that he fails to rule out a further possible account of what it is that he likes about his gustatory experiences while drinking Cabernet Sauvignon. Granting now that what he likes about those experiences is not just their content—this, by the way, is not obvious even putting aside the point above, since there will inevitably be a number of straightforward differences in content between the visual and gustatory cases (e.g., in the former, the relevant chemical property will be represented as being instantiated outside the mouth some distance away from Shoemaker's body)—and granting also that what he likes is not just that the experiences are produced by certain sense-organs, still it does not follow that what he really likes here are gustatory qualia. It seems to me reasonable to claim that what Shoemaker likes about the experiences is that they are gustatory experiences having a certain representational content. It is this package of content plus species that he finds so appealing—the presentation of a certain content in a certain mode of experience. In proposing this alternative, I am assuming that a sufficient condition for an experience's being gustatory is that it have an appropriate functional role.[15] Of course, this functional role is not given to one in introspection. Introspection, I maintain, reveals nothing about the inner nature of the property of being gustatory.[16] It merely informs one that the property is being tokened, just as, for example, it sometimes informs one that the properties of being a thought or being a desire are tokened.

We are now in a position to specify what it is that (1) asserts, when "this taste" is read opaquely, without appeal to qualia. In my view, (1) may be taken to say that what I like about certain experiences is that they represent a certain taste gustatorily, that is, that they are gustatory experiences representing that particular taste.

Shoemaker rejects this proposal of mine on the grounds that ". . . the way Cabernet Sauvignon tastes to me might change in such a way that, once I have accommodated to the change, my Cabernet Sauvignon–produced gustatory experiences have the same representational content as my earlier Cabernet Sauvignon–produced gustatory experiences did but are ones I find very unpleasant—and this might happen without my ceasing to like the way Cabernet Sauvignon *now* tastes to me."[17] I am not persuaded by this reply, however. If the way Cabernet Sauvignon tastes to me changes, the gustatory experiences it produces in me will, I claim, represent it as having a *different* taste from the one it had earlier. So, contra Shoemaker, there *will* be a change in the intentional content of my gustatory experiences.[18]

I conclude, then, that the Cabernet Sauvignon example can be handled without admitting that gustatory states have qualia.[19]

7.2.5 Blind "Sight"

Albert is a very remarkable man. He is blind and has been so since birth. Nevertheless, when he faces objects and concentrates fiercely, thoughts pop into his head—he knows not where they come from—about the visual properties and relations of the objects. These thoughts are so detailed that *content-wise* they are just as rich as the visual experiences sighted people have in the same circumstances. Indeed, were one to pay attention merely to the contents of Albert's thoughts, as expressed in his verbal descriptions of what is before him, one would be convinced that he is seeing. But Albert has no visual experiences. For Albert there is experientially no difference between his thoughts on such occasions and his thoughts when he ruminates on mathematics or art or life in general. In each case, thoughts just occur, and he is introspectively aware of no more than the contents of his thoughts. There is, then, an enormous felt difference between Albert and his sighted fellows at the times at which Albert seems to be seeing. This difference is one that Albert himself would come to appreciate in detail were he to gain sight. It is a difference that can only be explained on the assumption that Albert's inner states lack visual qualia.[20]

Not so. There is another explanation. In my view, what introspection tells me when I see something is not only the content of my visual experience but also the kind of experience it is. The crucial difference between Albert and myself when we face the same scene is that I am introspectively aware that I am undergoing a *visual experience* with a certain content, whereas Albert is introspectively aware that he is undergoing *thoughts* with that content. This difference is a felt difference—it is given in introspection—and it is why I, on the basis of my experience, believe that I am seeing something whereas Albert does not. What makes my experience visual is not, I maintain, its having certain visual qualia. After all, there is surely no short, straightforward list of the relevant qualia even if there are such entities as qualia. The property of being a visual experience is not itself classifiable as a visual quale either. For one thing, it is certainly not a property in virtue of which its tokens have their contents; for another, in my view, it is ontologically on a par with the properties of being a thought and being a desire. What is sufficient for my experience to be a *visual* experience is, I believe, that it have the right functional role.[21] Albert has no inner states that token *this* functional role but if he gains sight he will, and thereby he will come to appreciate what it was he lacked before.[22]

What the case of Albert does show, I think, is that the above-mentioned remarks of G. E. Moore about the visual experience of blue being diaphanous are in one respect inaccurate. When one introspects this experience, one is aware not only of the real color blue upon which it is directed but also of the fact that it is a visual experience. This is why in reporting what one is introspecting, one will say that one has a *visual experience* of blue. Were qualia presented to one on such occasions, there would surely be words to describe them. But our reports cite only the contents of our inner states and their species. Qualia are never mentioned.

7.2.6 The Inverted Spectrum

Tom has a very peculiar visual system. His visual experiences are systematically inverted with respect to those of his fellows. When Tom looks at red objects, for example, what it is like for him is the same as what it is like for other people when they look at green objects and vice versa. This peculiarity is one of which neither he nor others are aware. Tom has learned the meanings of color words in the usual way and he applies these words correctly. Moreover, his nonlinguistic behavior is standard.

Now when Tom views a tomato, say, in good light, his experience is phenomenally, subjectively different from the experiences you and I undergo. But his experience has the same representational content as ours. For his experience is the sort that is usually produced in him by viewing red objects and that usually leads him to believe that a red object is present. In viewing the tomato, then, he (like you and I) has an experience that represents the tomato as *red*.[23] The only way that Tom's experience can be subjectively different from yours and mine, then, is if it has a different visual quale. The intrinsic phenomenal quality in virtue of which his experience represents the tomato as red cannot be the one in virtue of which our experiences represent it as red. Rather, his is the one in virtue of which other experiences of ours represent grass and leaves, for example, as green.

One might respond to this argument by denying that a behaviorally undetectable inverted spectrum is possible.[24] There is another response available, however, that seems to me intuitively very satisfying. Contrary to what is claimed above, I believe that the difference between Tom and the rest of us when he views a tomato is that his experience, unlike ours, represents it as *green*. How is this possible? After all, the content of Tom's experience must be given to him, for the difference is a subjective one. But if the content is given to him, then he must be introspectively aware that his experience represents the tomato as green. Unfortunately, he is aware of no such thing. He sincerely asserts that the tomato is red and even that it looks red to him. Moreover, as was noted above, his experience is the sort that in him is typically produced by viewing red objects.

The answer, I maintain, is as follows: Introspection leads Tom astray. He forms a false belief about the content of his experience.[25] This content is certainly something *of* which he is introspectively aware, but it is a content that he misclassifies. He takes it to be the content *red*, and he therefore believes, on the basis of introspection, that he is undergoing an experience that represents red. In reality, his experience represents green. *This* representational difference is what is responsible for the subjective difference between his experience and ours. Tom's mistake is due, of course, to the fact that he is unaware of his peculiarity. He does not know that his visual system is producing experiences with atypical contents. He thinks he is normal, and he knows that the experience he undergoes in viewing the tomato is subjectively like those he undergoes in viewing other red objects. Therefore, he thinks that his experience represents red.

Perhaps it will be said that I haven't explained how Tom's experience can represent green when it is an experience of the subjective sort that is normally produced in him by viewing red objects, and that normally produces in him the belief that something red is present. My reply is that his experience is also of the subjective sort that is normally produced in people generally by viewing green objects, and that normally produces in them the belief that something green is present. Why should the former fact outweigh the latter in assessing what the content of his experience is? If we wish to pay equal attention to both facts, perhaps the most natural thing to say is that, relative to humans generally, Tom's experience represents green but, relative to him, it represents red. Since our experiences, on viewing the tomato, represent red relative to humans generally, there is, as before, a representational difference between Tom and us upon which to ground the subjective difference.

It is important to realize that I am not implicitly offering a reductive analysis of properties of the type "representing F (for group X)" in my comments above in terms of properties of the type "being of the subjective sort that is normally brought about (in group X) by viewing F objects" and so on. Since the relevant subjective sorts are, on my view, themselves properties of the type "being a visual sensation that represents F (for group X)," this would create a vicious circularity. I assume that properties such as representing green (for humans) have complex causal sufficient conditions, but I deny that these conditions require for their specification the concept of a subjective sort. This is easily illustrated by reference to the case of Tom.

In my view, visual experiences are constituted by brain states (see chapter 8). Thus, Tom's visual experience, when he views a tomato, has various intrinsic physical properties. Now since I deny that there are visual qualia, I deny that any of these properties are introspectively accessible. But I hold that among them is some property P that is normally tokened in humans generally as a result of their viewing green objects and that is normally caused in Tom as a result of his viewing red objects. Therefore, I hold that Tom's experience has the property of having an intrinsic physical property that is appropriately caused in the relevant populations by both red and green objects. This is sufficient, I claim, (in crude, first approximation and ignoring relevant effects of P) for Tom's experience to represent green relative to humans generally and red relative to Tom.[26]

It is important to realize that even given the population relativity of content, on the above approach, the property of representing F (for population X) cannot be identified with any of the intrinsic properties of the experiences that are its tokens. For the former property is both introspectively accessible and F-involving, whereas the latter properties are neither.

I want now to turn to another version of the inverted spectrum argument for visual qualia. Suppose that there is a species of creatures, half of whom have visual experiences that are the inverses of the experiences undergone by the other half. These differences arise as a result of naturally evolved differences in the retinas of the two groups. Surely, in this case, it is implausible to maintain that when two of the creatures (one from each group) view a tomato in good light, one has an experience that represents the tomato as green. But if both creatures' experiences represent the tomato as red, then the phenomenal difference in their experiences cannot be accounted for representationally. Hence, visual qualia must be postulated.

Once properties of the form representing so-and-so are taken to be population relative,[27] this argument loses its force. Both of the creatures' visual experiences represent the tomato as red *but only relative to their own groups*.[28] There is, then, a difference in content. Hence, the inverted spectrum still does not compel us to accept visual qualia.

The same conclusion holds, I maintain, for cases of intrasubjective inversion. If my visual apparatus is systematically tampered with so that objects that earlier looked red to me now come to look the way green objects used to look (and vice versa), my experiences will change from representing those objects as red to representing them as green (and vice versa). In this case, the relevant background population for these attributions of content is myself prior to the operation on my visual system.

Let us now move still farther afield from the commonplace realm.

7.2.7   Twin-Earth

Jones is watching a cat. On Putnam's planet Twin-Earth, Jones's doppelganger is watching a creature that looks just like a cat, but is genetically and biologically very different. Jones and Twin-Jones are subject to retinal images that exactly match and their brains are in exactly the same physicochemical states. Intuitively, then, their visual sensations are phenomenally identical. But the contents of their sensations are different. Since Twin-Jones has never seen or heard of cats (there aren't any cats on Twin-Earth, only twin-cats) and the beliefs he forms on the basis of his visual experiences are never of the type "This is a cat," Twin-Jones's experience represents not that there is a cat but rather that there is a twin-cat present. Hence, the phenomenal sameness obtaining between Jones's and Twin-Jones's visual experiences cannot be grounded in a sameness of content. Rather, it must be grounded in the experiences' sharing identical qualia.

This argument forgets that Twin-Jones's visual experience represents much more than just that a twin-cat is present. It also represents the location of the twin-cat relative to the viewer, its shape, color, orientation, and a myriad of other surface details. These aspects of the content of Twin-Jones's visual experience will also be found in the content of Jones's experience. I maintain that the phenomenal sameness obtaining between their visual experiences is traceable to these shared aspects.

It may seem that if our conception of the phenomenal is one that ties it to aspects of representational content, then we must reject the widely held view that subjective, phenomenal states of consciousness supervene on brain activity (as is implicitly supposed in the above Twin-Earth argument).[29] The matter is complex, however. The relevant aspects of content, as far as the phenomenal is concerned, are those that pertain to *directly* visible features, such as color and shape. If it is supposed that a visual experience that (relative to normal perceivers) represents red, say, is an experience that bears some natural relation R to normal perceivers and red objects, then, on my view, a person who lives in a world without red objects, and whose brain is artificially stimulated so that it is in exactly the same overall brain state as that of a normal human being on earth who is viewing a red object in daylight, will *not* be subject to a phenomenally identical visual experience. But if it is held instead that a visual experience that represents red (relative to normal perceivers) is an experience that, given normal perceivers, would bear relation R to them and red objects were there such objects, then, on my view, in the case just described, the absence of red objects will not generate the same result. On the former approach to content, then, my position requires a rejection of the thesis that physically identical brains *must* support phenomenally identical states of consciousness; but this is not required on the latter approach.

Which of the two approaches is to be preferred? It is evident that the latter will not do for *all* aspects of the content of visual experience; for, as applied to the earlier case of Jones, it entails the falsehood that Jones's experience represents not just a cat but also a twin-cat.[30] The former, however, seems intuitively too restrictive. Furthermore, both approaches make the dubious preliminary assumption that naturalistic necessary and sufficient conditions can be stated for the case of a visual experience's representing red. So, I am actually inclined to accept a weaker alternative, namely, that a visual experience represents red if, and only if, it stands in the representation relation to redness, whether or not redness is instantiated, relative to the appropriate perceivers. There is, I believe, a naturalistic *sufficient* condition associated with this of the sort I sketched earlier; but I do not believe that there is anything stronger. Nothing in this final approach entails that in a world without red objects *no* visual experiences (including those produced by artificial stimulation of the brain) will ever represent red. So I do not see that the phenomenal-neural supervenience thesis is directly threatened by my position.

7.2.8   Peacocke's Puzzle Cases

At the beginning of his book *Sense and Content,* Christopher Peacocke presents a number of ingenious cases designed to show that sensory experiences have qualia or, as he calls them, "sensational qualities."[31] Peacocke's first case is as follows: Suppose I view two trees of the same size, one twice as close as the other. My visual experience will represent the two trees as being of the same size—assuming, as will normally be the case, that the more distant tree does not really look smaller to me. But there is surely a sense in which the trees look different. This, according to Peacocke, can only be accounted for by supposing that the two trees have a different size in the visual field. And size in the visual field is, so Peacocke claims, a sensational quality or quale.

There is another possibility. The reason that the trees look different is, I believe, that it visually appears to me that if the trees were moved into line, the nearer one would completely obscure the other but not vice versa. This, in turn, is because my visual experience represents the nearer tree as being larger from here (the viewing position); that is, it represents it as subtending a larger visual angle. The difference Peacocke alleges to be due to different qualia, then, is, I maintain, due to aspects of the experience's representational content.

Peacocke rejects this proposal on the grounds that experiences like mine can be had by people who lack the concept of a visual angle. If, by this, Peacocke means to assert that people who lack the linguistic capacity to apply correctly the term "visual angle" or who have never heard of the term can have experiences like mine, then we may quickly agree. But it surely does not follow that *these* people cannot be subject to experiences that represent certain facts about visual angles. If Peacocke has something else in mind by the concept of a visual angle, then he must *show* (a) that lacking the concept precludes a person from undergoing a visual experience that represents anything about visual angles and (b) that lacking the concept does not preclude a person from undergoing an experience like mine. Without such a demonstration, it seems to me that Peacocke's first case is indecisive.

Peacocke's second case appeals to a contrast between binocular and monocular vision. If I view a situation with both eyes and then close an eye, things will appear different to me. This difference, according to Peacocke, is not representational. The one experience represents things as being just as they are represented as being by the other. Therefore, the difference must be due to a difference in qualia.

The claim I reject here (not surprisingly) is the claim that there is no representational difference. When I view the situation with both eyes, I see a little more of the objects and there is an increase in the determinacy of my representation of object distances. An appeal to qualia is not required.

Peacocke's third example is a case in which a wire cube is seen first as having one face in front of the other and then with the relative positions of the two faces reversed (see figure 7.1). Although there is a change in the experience here, something in the experience remains the same. This constant feature of the experience is, Peacocke maintains, a sensational quality.

The obvious response to this example is that the experience represents the cube as having a variety of unchanging spatial properties

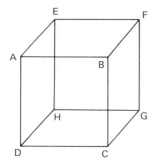

Figure 7.1
The Necker cube

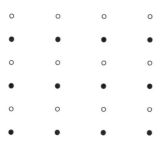

Figure 7.2

relative to the point of view and that this is really all that remains constant in the experience. For example, both before and after the "aspect" switch, side ABCD is represented as being lower than and somewhat to the left of side EFGH, side AEHD is represented as being level with and wholly to the left of side BFGC, and so on.

Other aspect switches are no more problematic for my position, I might add. Consider, for example, the following case (which Peacocke mentions a little later). We are to view the pattern shown in figure 7.2. We may see this pattern either with the dots running from the bottom to the top or with the dots running from the left to the right. How is this to be accounted for? Answer: There is a difference in content in the two experiences. Each experience represents the pattern as being composed of certain groups of dots. In the one case, the groups form columns; in the other, they form rows. It is because the experiences represent the pattern as falling into these groups that the perceiver will judge the pattern similar to figure 7.3 in the former instance, and similar to figure 7.4 in the latter.

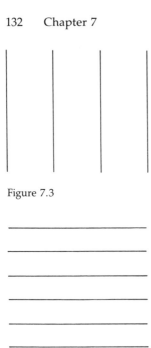

Figure 7.3

_____

_____

_____

_____

_____

_____

Figure 7.4

The overall conclusion I reach, then, is that there is no need to postulate visual qualia in order to account for the subjective aspects of our visual percepts and images. It suffices to admit that such percepts and images are visual and that they have contents. Qualia may be eliminated.

7.3   The Significance of the Elimination of Visual Qualia

Why does it matter whether visual qualia can be avoided? The answer, I suggest, is that the rejection of visual qualia not only makes certain aspects of visual experience less puzzling but also fits nicely with the account of imagistic representation presented in chapter 5. Let me explain, beginning with the former point.

Any adequate account of the subjective or phenomenal aspects of our visual states ought to yield an understanding of why those states have those aspects. Why, for example, does having a visual experience of blue "feel" the way it does and not some other way? It is hard to see how any satisfying answer can be given to this question, if the phenomenal aspects of such experiences derive from qualia.

Suppose, for example, that there are visual qualia and that such qualia are nonphysical and irreducible. Then the "felt" aspect of the visual experience of blue is a matter of its having a special, nonphysical property. It is the presence of this property that gives the visual experience its distinctive "feel." Does this really offer us any enlightenment? Apart from the usual concerns about the emergence and causal role of such properties, we may still wonder why the visual experience that has the content blue is associated with this irreducible felt quality rather than some other—why, for example, it does not have the felt quality of experiences that represent red. This surely is an impenetrable mystery.

Suppose now that visual qualia are physically reducible. Then the "felt" aspect of the visual sensation of blue is a matter of its having a certain physicochemical property. This is arguably an improvement on the above alternative—it dissolves any worry about the causal role of visual qualia, for example—but again it does not begin to explain why the visual experience that represents blue should "feel" as it does.

On the proposal I have made, there is a simple explanation. Introspection tells us that the visual experience that represents blue differs from the visual experience that represents red. This "felt" difference is, I claim, solely a matter of content. Since the colors represented by the two experiences are different, the experiences themselves are introspectively distinguishable. The reason, then, that the visual experience of blue "feels" as it does is that it could not "feel" any other way. The "felt" aspect simply cannot be divorced from the representational aspect.

I come finally to the issue of how the account of imagistic representation presented in chapter 5 itself counts against visual qualia. We saw earlier that, on the view I proposed, color gets represented in images via symbols that are located in cells of arrays that are themselves importantly like Marr's $2\frac{1}{2}$-D sketches. The color-representing symbols are here *parts* of imagistic representations: a given mental image will represent red, say, via its having, as a part, an appropriate symbol that represents red. Now visual qualia are intrinsic properties of mental images (or their parts) in virtue of which they represent what they do. Thus, if there are visual qualia, a given mental image will represent red via its having, or via some part of it having, an intrinsic property that represents red. Since a property of an image, or an image part, is certainly not itself a part, it follows that, on the account of imagistic representation I have elaborated, either (a) there are no visual qualia or (b) visual qualia are identical with properties of the sort "having such and such a symbol as a part" or "being such and such a symbol." The latter possibility seems indefensible, however. Why on earth should the presence of a given symbol within an imagistic representation confer upon the representation a distinctive phenomenal "feel"? After all, there are many symbol structures involved in cognition that have *no* subjective character at all. Once again, then, visual qualia are in trouble.[32]

The onus now lies with the advocate of qualia. I have tried to show that the rejection of visual qualia is defensible against a variety of objections and that it is not only intuitively satisfying but also well motivated. From the present perspective, it is not surprising that debates about the nature of visual qualia have not come to any clear resolution. The disputants in these debates have been trapped by a mistaken picture of visual experience, a picture that has led them to disagreements that lack any real substance.

Chapter 8

The Physical Basis of Imagery and the Causal Role of Image Content

Is a belt buckle typically longer than it is wide? What of a book? Does the letter "g" in its uppercase form have a long vertical stem? Questions such as these normally require the generation of mental images for their answer. In some of the earlier chapters, I brought out how the evidence from a variety of psychological experiments with normal subjects strongly suggests that the process of image generation is both sequential and constructive. In this chapter, one of the issues I want to look at concerns the location of this process. Is it really appropriate to speak of image generation as being physically realized in the brain? If so, is it highly localized within a single neural region or is it distributed across both hemispheres? And what of mental images themselves? Are there any a priori reasons to deny that mental images are physical? If not, is it more plausible to claim that images are strictly identical with brain processes or to take the slightly weaker view that images are constituted by such processes?

A further issue I want to address concerns the causal power of image content. It is basic to our ordinary conception of images that their contents play a role in producing behavior. For example, it is the fact that my image of a frog represents it as having no tail that is responsible for the image's causing me to answer the question "Do frogs have little, stubby tails?" negatively. How is it possible for image content to make a difference? This question is approached in the context of some recent philosophical discussions of the causal efficacy of mental content.

The chapter is divided into three sections. Sections 8.1 and 8.2 pertain to the physical basis of imagery; section 8.3 focuses on image content and its causal role.

8.1 The Physical Realization of Imagery in the Brain

Let me begin with the question of whether there are any compelling a priori reasons for denying that images are physical. It is evident that the failure of introspection to reveal the physical character of images in no way shows that images are nonphysical (any more than its failure to reveal the format of images—pictorial, descriptional, or otherwise—shows that they have no format). A more serious charge—one that I addressed in chapter 2—is that images, but not brain states, are sometimes pink or blue, for example. This does entail that images are not brain states. But the premise, on my view, is clearly false. Insofar as it is ever correct to talk of images as being pink or blue, what is meant, according to the position I defended in chapter 7, is that images sometimes represent the real-world colors pink and blue. Since representing pink and representing blue are things that brain states can accomplish straightforwardly, no properties have been adduced here that images have and brain states lack.

There are those who would insist that images cannot be brain states, since brain states may be located 2 or 3 inches from an ear, say, but it is unintelligible to attribute such a location to a mental image. The number of philosophers who are prepared to argue in this way is now very limited; and with good reason. Perhaps to some people it sounds odd to say that a mental image is 2 inches from an ear. But so what? No doubt it once sounded odd to assert that sound has a frequency or that light has a wavelength. That did not prevent it from turning out to be true. Furthermore, on the conception of mental images I have advocated, as interpreted symbol-filled arrays without any intrinsic visual qualia, there is obviously no conceptual problem with statements attributing specific spatial locations to images.

I see no a priori difficulties, then, with the view that mental images are physically realized in the brain. This is not to say, of course, that all, or indeed any, of their mental properties are neurophysiological. Consider, for example, the property of representing a cat. As we saw in the discussion of Twin-Earth in chapter 7, two people could be alike neurophysiologically and yet differ with respect to the instantiation of this property. Intentional properties, then, are not identical with, nor do they supervene on, neurophysiological properties.[1] Instead, they are best taken to be relational properties connecting states in the head to external objects and features.

Now if images are physical, then the process of image generation is physical too. But just where does this process occur? To make any headway with this question, we must turn away from a priori considerations to some interesting neuropsychological data.

L. G. Ungerleider and M. Mishkin have hypothesized that there are two higher-level visual systems in primates.[2] One of these—the ventral system—runs from area OC (primary visual cortex) through area TEO to the inferior temporal lobe (see figure 8.1). This system is concerned with the analysis of shape ("what"). The other system—the dorsal system—analyzes the location of the seen object ("where"). It runs from circumstriate area OB to OA and then on to PG (in the parietal lobe). The two systems together enable us to recognize objects when they appear in different positions in the visual field. The existence of these higher-level systems is shown, according to Ungerleider and Mishkin, by neuroanatomical investigations revealing two separate pathways, by neurophysiological investigations of the functions of cells in monkey brains, and by behavioral data obtained from animals with one or the other of the relevant neural regions surgically removed.

Stephen Kosslyn has argued[3] that the dorsal system—the one concerned with the analysis of location—is used to represent not only locations of objects in a scene but also, for separate encodings of object parts (formed during shifts of attention), relative locations of parts within a single object.[3a] If this is indeed the case, then shape information and information about spatial relations among parts are stored separately in the two systems. Thus, given that mental images are constructed by activating previously stored perceptual information, it is natural to suppose that there is a distinction between two sorts of processes that are used to generate mental images, namely, processes that draw on and activate information about shape (in the case of multipart images, information about part shape) and processes that use information about spatial relations among parts to

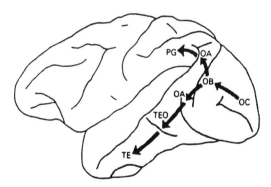

Figure 8.1
The dorsal and ventral systems of the primate brain. Reprinted, by permission, from M. Mishkin, L. G. Ungerleider, and K. A. Macko, "Object Vision and Spatial Vision: Two Cortical Pathways," *Trends in Neuroscience* (1983), p. 414.

arrange the parts correctly. Both Kosslyn and M. J. Farah have conducted experiments that support this hypothesis.[4] The experiments, which studied image generation in split-brain patients, lead to some general conclusions about the location of the image generation process in the brain.

Here is one of the experiments.[5] A commissurotomy patient, J. W., had lowercase letters from the alphabet visually presented on separate occasions to each hemisphere. In each case, J. W. was asked to judge whether the corresponding uppercase letter had any curved lines. The results were clear-cut: J. W.'s left hemisphere made no mistakes whatsoever, whereas his right hemisphere was correct only 65% to 70% of the time. What exactly does this show? Well, it was assumed that the task required imagery, and that the shapes of letters are stored in parcels of information about segments and categorical spatial relations (e.g., "above," "below," "connected to"). It was also assumed that *stored* information about categorical spatial relations is language-like and hence retained predominantly in the left hemisphere (for right-handed people it is known that the left hemisphere is better than the right at producing and using language). The conclusion indicated by the data and these assumptions, then, is that the process of arranging parts in an image by means of categorical spatial relations is more effective in the left hemisphere.[6]

This conclusion is bolstered by a variety of further data. For example, J. W. was also asked to perform tasks in which he was required to form images of single shapes without the use of any separate information about spatial relations. In this case, it was found that both hemispheres performed equally well. In another study, J. Deleval, J. De Mol, and J. Noterman[7] cite a patient whose power to form images was impaired by left-hemisphere damage and who described himself thus:

> When I try to imagine a plant, an animal, an object I can recall but one part, my inner vision is fleeting, fragmented; if I'm asked to imagine the head of a cow, I know that it has ears and horns, but I can't revisualize their respective places.

In an examination of the case study literature, Farah has also found that damage to the posterior left hemisphere is strongly correlated with loss of ability to generate multipart images.[8]

The hypothesis that the processes that arrange parts in images during image generation are restricted to the left hemisphere is too simple to account for all the data, however. The split-brain experiment on J. W. assumes that in the case of images of letters, image parts are arranged via information about categorical spatial relations.

But this cannot be the only information about spatial relations stored in the brain that is relevant to image generation. After all, any number of different images can be formed of a ball to the left of a wall, say, images in which the ball's distance from the wall varies. What is needed in some cases of image generation, then, is a process that arranges image parts in accordance with coordinate spatial information. Since the right hemisphere is better at representing and operating upon metric spatial information, one would expect this process to occur there. Experiments conducted by Kosslyn and his colleagues confirm this expectation.

Subjects were shown block letters and told to memorize how they appeared (see figure 8.2). Probe marks within the four corner brackets shown in this figure were then visually presented to each hemisphere, and the subjects were asked to judge whether the marks would fall on the letter, if it were within the brackets too (see figure 8.3). Kosslyn hypothesized that a process that utilizes coordinate spatial information to arrange parts is needed in this task, since fairly

Figure 8.2
Reprinted, by permission, from S. M. Kosslyn, "Aspects of a Cognitive Neuroscience of Mental Imagery," *Science* 240 (1988), pp. 1621–1625. © AAAS.

Figure 8.3
Reprinted, by permission, from S. M. Kosslyn, "Aspects of a Cognitive Neuroscience of Mental Imagery," *Science* 240 (1988), pp. 1621–1625. © AAAS.

precise information about segment locations is required to determine whether an imaged letter covers the X mark. Subjects were found to be faster at giving their responses when the brackets containing the probe were presented to the left visual field and thus were seen first by the right hemisphere.[9]

The overall conclusion I draw from the experiments I have briefly summarized is that image generation is a complex process, components of which can occur in both hemispheres. Some of the processes used to arrange image parts are more efficient in the left hemisphere and some are more efficient in the right. The upshot is that image generation is *not* a highly localized process occurring within a single neural region of a single hemisphere.

8.2 Identity versus Constitution

Most philosophers who accept that mental images are physical items believe that they are strictly identical with brain processes (or states). I want to argue that this is a mistake: images are best taken to be composed of or constituted by brain processes rather than strictly identical with them.

The word "is" in English sometimes expresses constitution instead of identity or predication. Consider, for example, the sentence "The house at 108 Bloom Road is just a dilapidated shack, but eighteen months from now, after we have completed renovations, it will be a very desirable residence." Were the word "is" in this sentence the "is" of strict identity, then the house referred to could not be altered and added on to while remaining the same house. To put the same point slightly differently, were the house strictly identical with a dilapidated shack and also strictly identical with a very desirable residence, then, by the symmetry and transitivity of identity, it would follow that a dilapidated shack is strictly identical with a very desirable residence. This is evidently false. Therefore, the house at 108 Bloom Road is not strictly identical with a dilapidated shack. Rather, it is today constituted by such a shack; eighteen months from now it will be constituted by something different, something that will then be a very desirable place to live.

In my view, the claim that mental images are brain processes is true only if the word "are" expresses constitution. My defense of this claim will be indirect. Suppose your lawnmower breaks down and you replace a faulty spark plug. Obviously, you still have the same lawnmower even though now it has a different part. Suppose now that your mower does not have a faulty plug. Still, it might have done so. Hence, it might have lost one of its actual parts and had it replaced by something else. It follows that the lawnmower in this case has a property that the sum of its (actual) parts does not, namely, the property of *possibly* lacking a particular spark plug.[10] Hence, by Leibniz's law,[11] the lawnmower is not strictly identical with the sum of its parts.

What is true here of the lawnmower is true, I believe, of everyday objects and events generally. A car is constituted by four wheels, an engine, a chassis. Each wheel is constituted by a tire, a hub, a hubcap. Likewise, a war is constituted by a number of battles. Each battle is constituted by certain actions. Each action is constituted by certain bodily movements. In none of these cases is there a strict identity.

Mental images, I maintain, are no different. Each mental image is constituted by a certain interpreted pattern of filled cells within an array of the sort I described in chapter 5. Each pattern, in turn, is constituted by certain brain processes (or states). Hence, each mental image is constituted by certain brain processes. This conclusion can be established without the second premise, I might add. So long as the relevant patterns are physically realized in the brain, it does not matter whether the relation is one of constitution or strict identity—in either case, given the first premise, the conclusion follows. What is needed, then, is a defense of the first premise.

Here is my defense. In some of the earlier chapters, we saw that mental images are subject to what Kosslyn calls "transformation processes"—processes such as rotation, scanning, and enlargement. What these processes do, on both Kosslyn's theory and my own, is to alter the pattern of filled cells in the visual buffer in various ways. They do not, however, destroy the mental images upon which they operate. When one scans across an image, for example, one still has the same image as before. What changes is the focus of one's attention.[12] Likewise, when one rotates an image in two dimensions, one does not, after rotation, have a second image. After all, one would surely not *describe* oneself here as having had *two* images. The rotated image is the same image as before: it merely represents the given object at a different orientation.

Consider, then, a particular mental image M. Suppose that M is not, in fact, subject to any of the above transformation processes. Still, it might easily have been. Had this occurred, some of M's component cells would have changed their contents and the overall pattern of filled cells would have been a different pattern. Hence, M has a modal property that the pattern lacks, namely, the property of *possibly* having such and such cells differently filled. Hence, M is not strictly identical with the pattern.

I have now completed my argument for the claim that it is a mistake to affirm that mental images are identical with brain processes. The relevant relation, in my view, is constitution, not identity.

8.3   The Causal Role of Image Content

How can the representational content of a mental image make a difference to behavior? This question has not received any significant attention in the recent philosophical literature; but it runs parallel to one that has been extensively discussed, namely the question of how the content of propositional attitudes (e.g., belief, memory, desire) can make a difference. The question concerning mental images can be divided into two further questions: (a) Given that there is a complete neurophysiological explanation of why any mental image has the behavioral effects it does (whether or not we ever manage to discover just what that explanation is), how can imagistic content play a causal role?; (b) Given that content is sometimes causally inert, as, for example, when saying things soothingly to my dog during a thunderstorm causes her to stop shaking (here it is not *what* I say that makes her relax but the tone of my voice), why is imagistic content causally efficacious with respect to behavior? Let me begin with (a).

I have claimed that mental images are physical items that are constituted by brain processes. I have also claimed that imagistic content is not itself a neurophysiological property but rather a relational property connecting images to external objects and features. Consider, then, a particular piece of behavior B, brought about by a certain mental image M. What is it about M that is responsible for its bringing about B? One answer goes as follows: M causes B in virtue of M's being constituted by a certain firing pattern F and F's having a specific physical property P. It is the fact that M is constituted by a firing pattern that has P that is responsible for M's causing B. Just how the firing pattern F leads to B will be filled out by the neurophysiologist. In gross outline, the story is that F, in virtue of having P, causes certain other firing patterns, the physical properties of which are responsible for their producing a certain firing pattern on the motor neurons. This, in turn, has physical features in virtue of which it produces electrical impulses in the nerves culminating in B.

In the sketch I just offered of how M brings about B, imagistic content played no role. There is, however, another possible explanation of what is responsible for M's bringing about B. To see this, suppose that B is my shuddering and M is an image I have of a tarantula crawling up my right leg. The ordinary, everyday explanation of why M produces B adverts to its content: M causes B because M has a content that produces a strong reaction of dislike, mixed with fear, and this reaction in turn produces shuddering. Now question (a) takes the neurophysiological explanation to threaten the ordinary, everyday explanation. If the neurophysiologist can, in principle, provide us with a complete physical account of what is responsible for M's causing B, how can there be any room for the folk psychological account? If M causes B in virtue of its having neural property P,[13] then how can M cause B in virtue of its having the property of representing a tarantula crawling up my leg (hereafter C)?[14]

It does not take an especially sensitive nose to detect what is wrong here. To say that M causes B in virtue of having P does not entail that M does not also cause B in virtue of having C. To suppose otherwise is to confuse "in virtue of" with "*only* in virtue of." Here is a nonpsychological example to illustrate this point. Benjamin Franklin signed the Declaration of Independence in Independence Hall, which is (and was) located in Philadelphia. Franklin signed the Declaration of Independence in Pennsylvania, then, in virtue of signing it in Independence Hall. Obviously, it does not follow from this that Franklin did not sign the Declaration of Independence in Pennsylvania in virtue of signing it in Philadelphia.[15]

Still, it might be objected that the example I have just given is importantly disanalogous to the case of M and its causing B. The properties in virtue of which Franklin signed the Declaration of Independence in Pennsylvania are related as follows: Franklin possessed the property of signing the Declaration of Independence in Philadelphia in virtue of his possessing the property of signing it in Independence Hall. The parallel claim in the case of M is that M has the property C in virtue of its having P. And this claim, it might be argued, is false. For Twin-Earth considerations of the sort discussed earlier establish that C does not supervene on any neurophysiological properties. The objection in a nutshell, then, is this: although it is true that M does not cause B either only in virtue of its having P or only in virtue of its having C, still if M does cause B in virtue of its having P and also in virtue of its having C, it had better be true additionally that M has C in virtue of having P.[16] Since C does not supervene on P, this last claim is *not* true. Hence, there remains a serious problem in supposing that image content is causally efficacious.

Not so. The fact that C does not supervene on any neurophysiological properties does not show that M does not have C in virtue of having P but merely that M does not have C only in virtue of having P. Consider, for example, the following case: I flip the switch *and thereby* I turn on the light. My action is both a switch flipping and a turning on of the light. It has the latter property T in virtue of its having the former property F. But T does not supervene on F; for it is not necessary that every action that has F has T. Hence, my action does not have T *only* in virtue of its having F. Rather, it is the fact that my action has F, together with various facts about the electrical connections between the switch and the light, that necessitates that my action has T. Exactly the same is true for M and the properties P and C. M has C in virtue of having P but not only in virtue of having P, since it is the possession of P, *together with* various facts about the external world and my relationship to it, that necessitates that M have C.

I conclude that neurophysiological explanations pose no threat whatsoever to the causal efficacy of imagistic content. I turn now to question (b). Let me begin with the example I mentioned earlier of speaking soothingly to my dog during a thunderstorm.

Here it is the tone of my utterances, not their content, that is causally efficacious. The sounds I produce cause a certain response in my dog in virtue of their tone and not in virtue of their content. With mental images, the situation intuitively is different. In this case, it *is* content that is efficacious. My image of a tarantula crawling up my right leg causes me to shudder in virtue of its content. Hence, the image has a certain causal property in virtue of its having a certain intentional property. But why should this be so?

If this question is taken to demand that a philosophical analysis be given of the locution "O has property P in virtue of having Q," together with a demonstration that images satisfy the specified conditions for the relevant causal and intentional properties, then I am very doubtful that it has an answer. For, although the above locution is a perfectly ordinary one, the correct use of which is easily illustrated by examples, it seems to me extremely unlikely that any interesting a priori analysis or definition of its meaning is possible. In this respect, talk of what it is for an object to have one property in virtue of having a second is in the same boat as most other ordinary talk. Indeed, it seems to me that not even the standard philosophical example of a term whose meaning may be specified in necessary and sufficient conditions—namely, the term "bachelor"—is really very plausible. What, after all, is a bachelor? One answer: an unmarried male. But what of a newborn male baby? Is he a bachelor? Surely not. So, perhaps we should say that a bachelor is an unmarried male of maturity. But then what of a man who was married but is now divorced, or a man who lives in a society that does not recognize the institution of marriage? What of the pope? Is he a bachelor? What about an unmarried man who has lived with the same woman for forty years, who has had several children with her, and whose finances are interwoven with hers? Less seriously, what about the case illustrated in figure 8.4?

In the face of examples such as these, one has three options: *either* dig one's heels in and attempt to defend the proposed analysis *or* admit that the concept of a bachelor is nothing like as simple as is usually supposed and add some further conditions *or* deny that the concept, in its ordinary usage, has necessary and sufficient conditions. I favor the final course. The first option is, I think, counterintuitive in at least some of the above cases. And the second option is always open to further counterexamples.

I take the same view with respect to the ordinary concept of what it is for an object to have a property in virtue of having another property.[17] Still, I am inclined to think that it is possible to formulate a *sufficient* condition for the truth of statements of the general form (1).

"I'm a bachelor myself."

Figure 8.4
Drawing by Drucker; © 1990. The New Yorker Magazine, Inc.

(1) O has the property of causing event E in virtue of having macroproperty P.

Since I also think that mental images satisfy the sufficient condition with respect to their contents and the appropriate causal properties, I maintain that we *can* have a more substantial account or explanation of why imagistic content is causally efficacious with respect to behavior.

I want to begin my attempt to formulate a satisfactory sufficient condition by considering the following proposal:

(2) O causes E in virtue of having macroproperty P if E has some property Q such that the instantiation of P is nomologically sufficient for the instantiation of Q.[18]

If (2) is to have any significant application outside the microphysical realm, it had better not be the case that the required nomological sufficiency be strict. Rather, I shall take it that so long as it is at least a law that P instances cause Q instances ceteris paribus, the condition of nomological sufficiency is met.

The thinking behind (2) is very straightforward. Normally when rocks strike windows, the windows shatter. We infer that the shattering occurs because of the impact of the rocks. In a few cases, however, rocks hit windows and the windows survive intact. This does not lead us to conclude that in those cases where the windows do shatter, the impact of the rocks is not responsible. Instead, we suppose that certain conditions that are met in these cases and that play a supporting role in the windows' breaking are not present in all cases. Hence, it is a law that windows shatter as a result of being struck by rocks ceteris paribus. And given this law, it follows that rocks cause windows to shatter in virtue of their striking them.

Folk psychology consists of a vast network of commonsense ceteris paribus laws connecting mental states with other mental states, external circumstances, and overt behavior. In those cases where the mental states have representational content, the laws advert to it. For example, it is a law that people who want something, and believe that a certain action is necessary in order to get it, will try to perform that action ceteris paribus. Similarly, it is a law that people who are asked questions about properties or aspects of things they have seen, and who have not thought about those properties or aspects much, will form images of the things before answering ceteris paribus.[19]

The theories of cognitive psychology are also made up of ceteris paribus laws. Cognitive psychologists try to explain the exercise of our cognitive capacities in terms of the interactions of inner representational states with one another, external circumstances, and overt behavior. As we have seen in earlier chapters, some of these inner states are accessible to consciousness, but many are not. The laws that cognitive psychologists formulate are based on experimental data concerning our cognitive capacities, and they typically make reference to the contents of the states that are hypothesized to constitute such capacities. Think, for example, of Shepard's claim that people who are shown pairs of block figures, and who are asked whether they are congruent, rotate images of the figures. Or consider Kosslyn's view that people generate images of complex figures part by part from representations stored in long-term memory of elements of the figures. These generalizations are evidently ceteris paribus, since there are occasional cognitive exceptions. Furthermore, the proper functioning of the imagery system can be affected by breakdowns at the physical level.

Now if (2) does indeed state a sufficient condition for the truth of statements of the form (1), then the existence of both folk and scientific laws that relate mental images to behavior, and that advert to their contents, supplies us with a firm foundation for the view that imagistic content is causally efficacious. Unfortunately, (2) is open to counterexamples. Little Tom ate some green raspberries and suffered indigestion as a result. It is a ceteris paribus law that eating green raspberries causes indigestion. But the raspberries clearly did not produce Tom's indigestion in virtue of their being green.[20]

In the face of counterexamples of this sort, it is tempting to propose an alternative to (2) along the following lines:

(3) O causes E in virtue of having macroproperty P if (a) there is some microproperty P' such that P supervenes on P', and (b) O causes E in virtue of having P'.[21]

(3) does better than (2) in the case of the raspberries. Since the microphysical property of raspberries upon which their greenness supervenes (that microproperty which is such that necessarily, for any time t, anything having it at t is green at t) is not a property in virtue of which raspberries produce indigestion, (3) does not entail that the greenness of the raspberries was causally efficacious with respect to Tom's indigestion. (3) also conforms well with many other cases of macrocausation. But it too is open to counterexamples.

The thief entered loudly and thereby awakened everyone in the house. In other words, the entrance of the thief, in virtue of being loud, caused the household's awakening. Now being loud suffices for making more noise than a falling leaf or having an IQ of 170. Hence, the microproperty of the thief's entrance upon which being loud supervenes is also a property upon which making more noise than a falling leaf or having an IQ of 170 supervenes. But it seems *highly* counterintuitive to say that the thief's entrance, in virtue of making more noise than a falling leaf or having an IQ of 170, caused the awakening of the entire household.

This problem case presents no difficulty for (2) since it is obviously not a law that entrances that make more noise than falling leaves or have IQs of 170 awaken whole households. The thought occurs, then, to put (2) and (3) together to produce the following sufficient condition:

> (4) *O* causes *E* in virtue of having macroproperty *P* if (a) *E* has some property *Q* such that the instantiation of *P* is nomologically sufficient for the instantiation of *Q*; (b) there is some microphysical property *P'* such that *P* supervenes on *P'*; and (c) *O* causes *E* in virtue of having *P'*.[22]

I know of no counterexamples to (4).[23] But there are plenty of macrocausal transactions that do not meet the specified sufficient condition. Suppose, for example, you treat your geraniums with a certain fertilizer. Intuitively, your action, in virtue of being an application of this particular fertilizer (call it "*F*"), causes the geraniums to grow dramatically. Subsequent chemical analysis reveals that, of the five chemical components of *F*, only three are active. It follows that the microphysical property upon which the property of being an application of *F* supervenes has components that are causally irrelevant to the growth of the geraniums. Hence, clause (c) in (4) is not met.[24]

Cases like the one I have just described can be accommodated easily enough by a small revision in clause (c). Instead of requiring that *O* cause *E* in virtue of having microproperty *P'*, we may demand more weakly that *O* causes *E* in virtue of having some microproperty that *P'* includes. Here I assume that one property includes another if, and only if, the former is a conjunctive property having the latter as a conjunct.

The sufficient condition we have finally arrived at has broad application to everyday causal transactions. More importantly for our purposes it supports the claim that imagistic content is causally efficacious with respect to behavior. For images certainly bear the contents they do *in part* because of the instantiation of appropriate intrinsic microphysical properties within the brain. These properties enter into complex causal connections with other externally based microphysical properties and thereby contents are determined. Thus, given that the former microphysical properties are causally relevant to the behavior images elicit, clause (c) is satisfied. Since the other clauses are satisfied too, (4) in its revised form yields the result that images cause behavior in virtue of their contents.

That completes my study of mental images. I have tried to present a useful survey of work on imagery, both historical and contemporary. I have also tried to combine philosophical and psychological perspectives within a single comprehensive theory. The position I have developed, even though it runs counter to a number of orthodoxies, is, I believe, not only intuitively pleasing but also scientifically plausible. There is, to be sure, more to imagery than meets the eye; but much of what was mysterious is now, I hope, intelligible.

Appendix

The following is a program (in MBASIC) that displays an image (in this case, a line) on a computer monitor and then rotates it 360 degrees in 45-degree increments. The data defining the image are stored as a list of descriptional elements in a disk file. The program takes these data as input and stores them in a quasi-pictorial array in the computer's memory. This array is then used by the program to produce a picture of a rotating line on the screen. (NOTE: The physical configuration of the data file on the disk need not mirror that of the presentation given below. Furthermore, the physical locations of the cells of the quasi-pictorial array in the computer's memory need not be contiguous.)

10	REM:	IMAGE ROTATION PROGRAM
20	DIM A$(5,5)	Set up array to hold image data
30	DIM H$(5,5)	Set up holding array
40	OPEN "I",#1, "IMAGE"	Open file containing image data for input
50	For J=1 TO 25	
60	INPUT #1, W$	Input item from file
70	X=VAL(LEFT$(W$,1))	Read X coordinate from item
80	Y=VAL(MID$(W$,2,1))	Read Y coordinate from item
90	Z$=MID$(W$,3,1)	Read content of cell from item
100	A$(X,Y)=Z$	Put Z$ in cell X,Y of array
110	NEXT J	
120	CLOSE	Close data file
130	FOR J=1 TO 8	
140	GOSUB 1000	Display image on monitor
150	GOSUB 2000	Rotate data 45 degrees
160	NEXT J	

```
170      GOSUB 1000
180      END
1000     REM:                       IMAGE DISPLAY
                                    SUBROUTINE
1010     PRINT CHR$(26)             Clear screen
1020     FOR X=1 TO 5
1030     FOR Y=1 TO 5
1040     PRINT A$(X,Y) + " ";       Display cell X,Y
1050     NEXT Y
1060     PRINT
1070     NEXT X
1080     RETURN
2000     REM:                       DATA ROTATION
                                    SUBROUTINE
2010     GOSUB 3000                 Shift data in outer cells into
                                    holding array
2020     GOSUB 4000                 Shift data in inner cells into
                                    holding array
2030     FOR X=1 TO 5               Load shifted data from
                                    holding array into main
                                    array
2040     FOR Y=1 TO 5
2050     A$(X,Y)=H$(X,Y)
2060     NEXT Y
2070     NEXT X
2080     RETURN
3000     REM:                       OUTER CELL SHIFT
                                    SUBROUTINE
3010     FOR K=1 TO 3:H$(1,K+2)=A$(1,K):H$(K+2,5)=
         A$(K,5): NEXT K
3020     H$(2,5)=A$(1,4)
3030     H$(5,4)=A$(4,5)
3040     FOR K=5 TO 3 STEP −1:H$(5,K−2)=A$(5,K):
         H$(K−2,1)=A$(K,1):NEXT K
3050     H$(4,1)=A$(5,2)
3060     H$(1,2)=A$(2,1)
3070     RETURN
4000     REM:                       INNER CELL SHIFT
                                    SUBROUTINE
4010     FOR K=2 TO 3:H$(2,K+1)=A$(2,K):H$(K+1,4)=
         A$(K,4):NEXT K
```

```
4020      FOR K=4 TO 3 STEP −1:H$(4,K−1)=A$(4,K):
          H$(K−1,2)=A$(K,2):NEXT K
4030      RETURN
```

The contents of the data file for a vertical line might be as follows:

```
11-,12-,13*,14-,15-
21-,22-,23*,24-,25-
31-,32-,33*,34-,35-
41-,42-,43*,44-,45-
51-,52-,53*,54-,55-
```

The line is indicated by the asterisks; the hyphens provide a background within which it is rotated. The order of the elements separated by commas is irrelevant since each element contains the coordinates of the cell into which the hyphen or asterisk is to be placed.

Although the program has been designed to take descriptional data as input, it would have been more natural to have stored it on disk in quasi-pictorial form. Had this been done, steps 40 through 120 could have been replaced with the following:

```
40     OPEN "I",#1, "IMAGE"     Open file containing image
                                data for input
50     FOR J=1 TO 5
60     FOR K=1 TO 5
70     INPUT #1, W$             Input item from file
80     A$(J,K)=W$               Put W$ in cell J,K of array
90     NEXT K
100    NEXT J
110    CLOSE
```

The contents of the data file would have been as follows:

```
-,-,*,-,-
-,-,*,-,-
-,-,*,-,-
-,-,*,-,-
-,-,*,-,-
```

Since the order in which the elements are read from the program determines the location in the quasi-pictorial array, there is no need to include the array addresses in the file.

Notes

Chapter 1

1. Aristotle, *On the Soul*, 427b 19.
2. Aristotle, *On Memory and Recollection*, 451a 19.
3. Aristotle, *On the Soul*, 427b 22.
4. See, for example, *On Memory and Recollection*, 450a 1. In some translations this reads as follows: "Now we have already discussed imagination in the treatise *On the Soul* and we concluded there that thought is impossible without an image."
5. See, for example, Martha Nussbaum, *De Motu Animalium* (Princeton, 1978).
6. See Rene Descartes, *Meditations on First Philosophy*, in *The Philosophical Works of Descartes*, trans. by Elizabeth Muldane and G. R. T. Ross (Cambridge: Cambridge University Press, 1968), pp. 185–186.
7. Descartes, *Meditations on First Philosophy*, p. 159.
8. Descartes, *Meditations on First Philosophy*, p. 160.
9. Thomas Hobbes, *Leviathan Parts I and II* (New York: Liberal Arts Press, 1958), p. 27.
10. Hobbes, *Leviathan*, p. 28.
11. Hobbes, *Leviathan*, p. 28.
12. This interpretation is suggested by Hobbes's comments on motions in the "internal parts of a man" when "he sees, dreams, etc." See Hobbes, *Leviathan*, p. 27.
13. See John Locke, *An Essay Concerning Human Understanding*, bk. II, chaps. 1–13; also bk. III, chaps. 1–3.
14. Locke, *Essay Concerning Human Understanding*, bk. II, chap. 10, sec. 2.
15. Locke, *Essay Concerning Human Understanding*, bk. III, chap. 3, sec. 7.
16. Locke, *Essay Concerning Human Understanding*, bk. II, chap. 8, sec. 7.
17. Locke, *Essay Concerning Human Understanding*, bk. II, chap. 11, sec. 9.
18. See Ludwig Wittgenstein, *The Blue and Brown Books* (New York: Harper and Row, 1958), p. 12.
19. George Berkeley, *The Principles of Human Knowledge*, sec. 19.
20. Berkeley, *Principles of Human Knowledge*, sec. 10.
21. Berkeley, *Principles of Human Knowledge*, sec. 13.
22. Compare Jonathan Bennett, *Locke, Berkeley, and Hume: Central Themes* (Oxford: Clarendon Press, 1971), p. 37.
23. David Hume, *A Treatise of Human Nature*, bk. I, pt. 4, sec. 6.
24. Hume, *Treatise of Human Nature*, bk. I, pt. 1, sec. 7.
25. Immanuel Kant, *Critique of Pure Reason*, trans. by Norman Kemp Smith (New York: St. Martin's Press, 1965), bk. II, A 141, p. 182.
26. Nelson Goodman, *The Languages of Art* (London: Oxford University Press, 1968), p. 4. I might add that Goodman holds not only that resemblance is not sufficient

for pictorial representation but also that it is not necessary. See Goodman, *Languages of Art*, pp. 3–31.

27. Ludwig Wittgenstein, *Philosophical Investigations* (New York: Macmillan, 1953), p. 54.

28. This point is well made by Ned Block in his "Mental Pictures and Cognitive Science," *The Philosophical Review* 92 (1983), pp. 499–541.

29. See C. W. Perky, "An Experimental Study of Imagination," *American Journal of Psychology* 21 (1910), pp. 422–452.

30. See James Lackner and Merrill Garrett, "Resolving Ambiguity: Effects of Biasing Context in the Unattended Ear," *Cognition* 1 (1973), pp. 359–372.

31. See Richard Nisbett and Timothy Wilson, "Telling More than We Can Know: Verbal Reports on Mental Proceses," *Psychological Review* 84 (1977), pp. 231–259.

32. See Nisbett and Wilson, "Telling More than We Can Know."

33. For further experimental evidence in support of this claim, see R. Nisbett and L. Ross, *Human Inference: Strategies and Shortcomings of Social Judgment* (Englewood Cliffs, N.J.: Prentice-Hall, 1980).

34. See W. Wundt, *Lectures on Human and Animal Psychology*, trans. by S. E. Creighton and E. B. Tichner (New York: Macmillan, 1894).

35. See O. Kulpe, *Outlines of Psychology*, trans. by E. B. Tichner (New York: Macmillan, 1909).

36. See J. B. Watson, "Psychology as the Behaviorist Views It," *Psychological Review* 20 (1913), pp. 158–177.

Chapter 2

1. See G. E. Moore, *Philosophical Studies* (London and New York, 1922); H. H. Price, *Perception* (London: Methuen, 1964); Bertrand Russell, *The Problems of Philosophy* (London, 1912).

2. See Gilbert Ryle, *The Concept of Mind* (New York: Barnes and Noble, 1949), pp. 246–251.

3. See Ryle, *Concept of Mind*, pp. 265–266. See also John Heil, "Mental Imagery and Mystification," *The Behavioral and Brain Sciences* 2 (1979), p. 555.

4. See Ryle, *Concept of Mind*, pp. 252–253.

4a. I am not here endorsing this analysis.

5. See, for example, J. M. Shorter, "Imagination," *Mind* 61 (1952), pp. 528–542.

6. See Jerry Fodor, "Imagistic Representation," in *Imagery*, ed. by Ned Block (Cambridge, Mass.: MIT Press, 1982), p. 78.

7. See Daniel Dennett, "The Nature of Images and the Introspective Trap," in Block, *Imagery*, pp. 54–55.

8. See J. J. C. Smart, "Sensations and Brain Processes," *The Philosophical Review* 68 (1959), pp. 141–156.

9. For more on this view, see chapter 7.

10. My own position here is that there are no such qualities for color words to express. See chapter 7.

11. See Watson, "Psychology as the Behaviorist Views It"; also *The Ways of Behaviorism* (New York: Harper, 1928).

12. Watson, *Ways of Behaviorism*, pp. 75–76.

13. For a good summary of the reasons for this decline, see Stephen Kosslyn, *Ghosts in the Mind's Machine* (New York: W. W. Norton, 1983), pp. 9–11.

14. See Locke, *Essay Concerning Human Understanding*, bk. II, chap. 8, sec. 7. I am not suggesting, incidentally, that Locke overall was a descriptionalist on imagery. See my comments in chapter 1.

15. Advocates of this thesis typically limit themselves to visual images, but it is sometimes suggested that other images (e.g., auditory images) represent in like manner.

16. Strictly speaking, descriptionalism does not require physicalism with respect to images. However, I know of no descriptionalist who holds that mental images are nonphysical entities.

17. See, for example, Dennett, "Nature of Images," pp. 51–61; Shorter, "Imagination"; Zenon Pylyshyn, "Imagery and Artificial Intelligence," in *Readings in the Philosophy of Psychology*, vol. 2, ed. by Ned Block (Cambridge, Mass.: Harvard University Press, 1981); also "The Imagery Debate," in Block, *Imagery*, pp. 151–206.

18. See Shorter, "Imagination."

19. See Dennett, "Nature of Images."

20. A parallel response is available to the defender of the pictorial view of images against the charge that inner pictures require inner eyes, if he or she adopts Stephen Kosslyn's elaboration of the view (presented in chapter 3).

21. See, for example, Kim Sterelny, "The Imagery Debate," *Philosophy of Science* 53 (1986), pp. 560–583.

22. See, for example, Hartry Field, "Mental Representation," *Erkenntnis* 13 (1978); J. Fodor, "Propositional Attitudes," *The Monist* 61 (1978); W. Lycan, "Toward a Homuncular Theory of Believing," *Cognition and Brain Theory* 4 (1982).

23. For a detailed discussion of the semantic and metaphysical foundations of the adverbial approach, see Michael Tye, "The Adverbial Approach to Visual Experience," *The Philosophical Review* 93 (1984), pp. 195–225; also Michael Tye, *The Metaphysics of Mind* (New York: Cambridge University Press, 1989).

24. See, for example, Bruce Aune, *Knowledge, Mind, and Nature* (New York: Random House, 1967), pp. 147–148; R. M. Chisholm, *Perceiving* (Ithaca, N.Y.: Cornell University Press, 1957), pp. 115–125; and *Person and Object* (LaSalle, Ill.: Open Court, 1976), pp. 46–52; Wilfrid Sellars, "Phenomenalism," in *Science, Perception, and Reality* (London: Routledge and Kegan Paul, 1963), pp. 92–95; and *Science and Metaphysics* (London: Routledge and Kegan Paul, 1968), pp. 9–28; Michael Tye, "Adverbial Approach to Visual Experience" and *Metaphysics of Mind*.

25. For a discussion of this issue, see Tye, *Metaphysics of Mind*, chap. 8.

26. See Richard Rorty, "Mind-Body Identity, Privacy, and Categories," *Review of Metaphysics* 19 (1965); Paul Churchland, *Scientific Realism and the Plasticity of Mind* (New York: Cambridge University Press, 1979).

Chapter 3

1. For a summary of Kosslyn's work, see his *Image and Mind* (Cambridge, Mass.: Harvard University Press, 1980); also his *Ghosts in the Mind's Machine* (New York: W. W. Norton, 1983).

2. See Ned Block, "Mental Pictures and Cognitive Science," *The Philosophical Review* 92 (1983), pp. 499–541.

3. See Hubert L. Dreyfus and Stuart E. Dreyfus, *Mind over Machine* (New York: The Free Press, 1986).

4. See, for example, Kosslyn, *Ghosts in the Mind's Machine*, p. 22.

5. Actually, even this claim is too strong. Distortions of one sort or another can be accommodated by weakening the stated requirement so that it obtains only in a sufficient number of cases and only when P_1, P_2, and P_3 do not appear to be at different distances away.

6. I have chosen a minimally different figure from the one that Kosslyn himself presents. Kosslyn's position is to be found in *Ghosts in the Mind's Machine*, pp. 22–25.

7. Kosslyn, *Ghosts in the Mind's Machine*, p. 23.

7a. I ignore here in condition (iii) complications presented by the third dimension. See chapter 5 for a discussion of the representation of depth in quasi-pictures.

8. For a discussion of one possible nonspatial interpretation of "part," see Michael Tye, "Representation in Pictorialism and Connectionism," *Southern Journal of Philosophy,* supplement containing proceedings of the Spindel Conference on Connectionism, vol. 26 (1988), pp. 163–183.

9. Stephen Kosslyn, "The Medium and the Message in Mental Imagery," in Block, *Imagery,* p. 217.

10. Kosslyn, "Medium and Message," p. 215. The parenthetical phrases in the two quoted passages are mine.

11. This conclusion rests on the assumption that the representational parts of a representation lie spatially within that representation. Without this assumption it could be denied that the tokens of "filled" are representationally simple.

12. See, for example, *Ghosts in the Mind's Machine*, p. 23.

13. See, for example, "Medium and Message," pp. 213–214.

14. For a defense of this hypothesis, see Kosslyn, *Image and Mind.* See also section 3.3 below.

15. See Block, "Mental Pictures and Cognitive Science," pp. 516–517.

16. Kosslyn has not modeled this process in detail. For an account of pattern recognition processes that seems applicable here, see S. Ullman, "Visual Routines," *Cognition* 18 (1984), pp. 97–159.

17. Block, Introduction to *Imagery,* p. 4.

18. Block, "Mental Pictures and Cognitive Science," p. 535.

19. Dreyfus and Dreyfus, *Mind over Machine,* p. 90.

20. Kosslyn, *Ghosts in the Mind's Machine*, p. 23. The same view is also explained in his *Image and Mind,* p. 33.

21. Kosslyn, *Ghosts in the Mind's Machine*, p. 23.

22. This appendix was prepared by William Tolhurst.

23. So these processes, for Kosslyn, are *not* analogue processes in the sense of being mathematically continuous. But they are analogue in another, weaker sense. See the discussion of scanning and rotation in section 3.3.

24. It is interesting to note that when subjects were asked to imagine the background colors as well as the stripes, they did not show any McCollough effect: no tingeing of the pattern of horizontal and vertical stripes resulted. For more on the McCollough effect in imagery, see R. A. Finke and M. J. Schmidt, "Orientation-Specific Color Aftereffects following Imagination," *Journal of Experimental Psychology: Human Perception and Performance* 3 (1977), pp. 599–606.

25. See R. N. Shepard and P. Podgorny, "Cognitive Processes That Resemble Perceptual Processes," in *Handbook of Learning and Cognitive Processes,* ed. by W. K. Estes (Hillsdale, N.J.: Erlbaum, 1978).

26. See E. Bisiach and G. R. Luzzatti, "Unilateral Neglect of Representational Space," *Cortex* 14 (1978), pp. 129–133.

27. Kosslyn sometimes writes as if he thinks that the inspection processes involved in imagery and visual perception are *all* the same. This stronger position is difficult to reconcile with neuropsychological data pertaining to subjects who are unable to recognize, on the basis of their percepts, visually presented objects but who nonetheless have unimpaired imagery. See here, e.g., J. M. Nielsen, *Agnosia, Apraxia, Aphasia: Their Value in Cerebral Localization* (New York: Hafner, 1962). For

a good general discussion of the links between imagery and visual perception, see Ronald A. Finke, "Mental Imagery and the Visual System," *Scientific American*, March 1986, pp. 88–95.

28. See Kosslyn, *Image and Mind;* Kosslyn, "Medium and Message," pp. 207–245; S. M. Kosslyn, S. Pinker, G. Smith, and S. Shwartz, "On the Demystification of Mental Imagery," in Block, *Imagery*, pp. 131–150.

29. Kosslyn, *Image and Mind*, p. 141.

30. See Kosslyn, "Medium and Message" and Kosslyn et al., "Demystification of Mental Imagery."

31. See R. Finke and S. Pinker, "Spontaneous Imagery Scanning in Mental Extrapolation," *Journal of Experimental Psychology: Learning, Memory, and Cognition* 2 (1982), pp. 142–147.

32. See, for example, Kosslyn et al., "Demystification of Mental Imagery." Also see S. M. Kosslyn et al., "Response to Open Peer Commentary," *The Behavioral and Brain Sciences* 2 (1979), p. 573.

33. See Kosslyn et al., "Response to Open Peer Commentary," p. 573.

34. Kosslyn et al., "Response to Open Peer Commentary," p. 573.

35. See Kosslyn, *Image and Mind*, chap. 8.

36. See R. N. Shepard and N. Metzler, "Mental Rotation of Three-dimensional Objects," *Science* 171 (1971), pp. 701–703.

37. Described in R. N. Shepard and L. Cooper, *Mental Images and Their Transformations* (Cambridge, Mass.: MIT Press, 1982), pp. 59–62.

38. See Lynn Cooper and Roger Shepard, "Turning Something Over in the Mind," *Scientific American* 251 (1984), p. 114.

39. See M. J. Farah, K. M. Hammond, D. N. Levine, and R. Calvano, "Visual and Spatial Mental Imagery: Dissociable Systems of Representation," *Cognitive Psychology* 20 (1988), pp. 439–462.

40. See M. Farah, "The Neurological Basis of Mental Imagery: A Componential Analysis," *Cognition* 18 (1984), pp. 245–272.

41. See Kosslyn, *Image and Mind*, pp. 347–406; also "Medium and Message," pp. 223–224.

42. Compare S. Pinker, "Visual Cognition: An Introduction," *Cognition* 18 (1984), pp. 54–55.

Chapter 4

1. A *necessary* condition for counting one linguistic type, L_1, a part of another, L_2, is that L_1 is tokened whenever L_2 is tokened.

2. Kosslyn, *Image and Mind*, p. 29.

3. Zenon Pylyshyn, "Imagery and Artificial Intelligence," in *Readings in Philosophy of Psychology*, vol. 2, ed. by Ned Block (Cambridge, Mass.: Harvard University Press, 1981), pp. 170–194; also "The Imagery Debate: Analog Media versus Tacit Knowledge," *Psychological Review* 88 (1981), pp. 16–45.

4. See Pylyshyn, "The Imagery Debate."

5. See C. L. Richman, D. B. Mitchell, and J. S. Reznick, "Mental Travel: Some Reservations," *Journal of Experimental Psychology: Human Perception and Performance* 5 (1979), pp. 5–13.

6. See Kosslyn, *Image and Mind*, pp. 459–460.

7. See Kosslyn, *Image and Mind*, pp. 459–460.

8. See R. A. Finke, "Levels of Equivalence in Imagery and Perception," *Psychological Review* 87 (1980), pp. 113–139.

9. See S. Kosslyn, T. Ball, and B. Reiser, "Visual Images Preserve Metric Spatial Information: Evidence from Studies of Image Scanning," *Journal of Experimental Psychology: Human Perception and Performance* 4 (1978), pp. 47–60.

10. See Zenon Pylyshyn, "The Role of Location Indexes in Spatial Perception: A Sketch of the FINST Spatial-Index Model," *Cognition* 32 (1989), pp. 65–97.

11. See Pylyshyn, "Location Indexes in Spatial Perception," p. 91.

12. See Zenon Pylyshyn, "The Rate of 'Mental Rotation' of Images: A Test of a Holistic Analogue Hypothesis," *Memory and Cognition* 7 (1979), pp. 19–28.

13. See Pylyshyn, "Imagery and Artificial Intelligence," pp. 174–176.

14. See Pylyshyn, "Imagery and Artificial Intelligence," p. 176.

15. Hinton's view is presented in his "Some Demonstrations of the Effects of Structural Descriptions in Mental Imagery," *Cognitive Science* 3 (1979), pp. 231–250; also "Imagery without Arrays," *Behavioral and Brain Sciences* 2 (1979), pp. 555–556.

16. For a discussion of generalized cones, see D. Marr, *Vision* (San Francisco: W. H. Freeman, 1982), pp. 223–225.

17. What is true in this case is also true in a wide variety of cases.

18. One well-known and important account of vision that appeals to such descriptions is Marr and Nishihara's theory, presented in Marr, *Vision*. See also my discussion in chapter 5.

19. Compare Pinker, "Visual Cognition: An Introduction," p. 19.

20. See, for example, Hinton, "Imagery without Arrays."

21. Contra Hinton, I do not believe that this objection is decisive. See my comments in chapter 5.

Chapter 5

1. See Marr, *Vision*.

2. Marr's position here is compatible with the claim that the retinal image is reconstructed in the visual cortex; for zero-crossings may be found indirectly by processes that examine the retinotopic representation.

3. S. W. Kuffler, "Discharge Patterns and Functional Organization of the Mammalian Retina," *Journal of Neurophysiology* 16 (1953), pp. 37–68.

4. See Marr, *Vision*, pp. 64–66.

5. See D. Hubel and T. Wiesel, "Brain Mechanisms of Vision," in *The Brain: A Scientific American Book* (New York: W. H. Freeman, 1979).

6. Psychophysical experiments add further empirical support to Marr's view. This work establishes that there are several different spatial frequency channels or operators in vision. See, for example, C. Blakemore and F. Campbell, "On the Existence of Neurons in the Human Visual System Selectively Sensitive to the Orientation and Size of Retinal Images," *Journal of Physiology* 203 (1969), pp. 237–260.

7. Measuring binocular disparity is not as easy as one might first think. The visual system must first match the appropriate parts of the retinal projections and, given the disparities between the two images, it will not help to examine the same place on each retina.

8. Marr, *Vision*, p. 272. On Marr's view, then, early vision is a distinct module.

9. Still, it might be argued that the matching process envisaged here will take too long, given the relatively long time it takes neurons to fire (tens of milliseconds) and the fact that human recognition of *what* is seen typically takes less than 1 second. For a response to arguments of this sort (i.e., arguments relying on the "one hundred step" rule), see J. Fodor and Z. Pylyshyn, "Connectionism and Cognitive Architecture: A Critical Analysis," *Cognition* 28 (1988), pp. 3–71.

10. I support this claim in section 5.4 below and in chapter 6.

11. See Pinker, "Mental Imagery and the Third Dimension," *Journal of Experimental Psychology: General* 109 (1980), pp. 354–371.

12. See Kosslyn, *Ghosts in the Mind's Machine*, p. 157.

13. It is interesting to note that in Shepard and Metzler's experiment on the rotation of representations of block figures (representations produced by physically present stimuli as opposed to memory representations), rotation in the third dimension was found to be no slower than rotation in two dimensions.

14. This model has been advocated by, for example, F. Attneave, "Representations of Physical Space," in *Coding Processes in Human Memory*, ed. by A. Melton and E. Martin (Washington, D.C.: V. H. Winston, 1972).

15. See "Mental Imagery and the Third Dimension."

16. In, for example, *Ghosts in the Mind's Machine*.

17. For a discussion of cases of impaired imagery in which such systems malfunction, see Michael Tye, "Image Indeterminacy: The Picture Theory of Images and the Bifurcation of 'What' and 'Where' Information in Higher Level Vision," forthcoming.

18. So, we can here fail to notice anything about the direction of *A* to *B*. It is one thing to have, in vision, a unified visual percept *of* two objects. It is another to cognitively process information in the percept about relative direction, and hence to see *that* their relative direction is so-and-so.

19. See Finke and Pinker, "Spontaneous Imagery Scanning."

20. See S. Kosslyn et al., "Demystifying Imagery—Response to Commentators," *Behavioral and Brain Sciences* 2 (1979), p. 573.

21. Kosslyn et al., "Demystifying Imagery—Response to Commentators," p. 573. Thus, contra Pylyshyn's understanding of his view, Kosslyn is happy to grant that the rate of rotation of images can vary. For more on this topic, see section 5.4 below.

22. For the reasons I gave in chapter 4, I find the attempt to explain the data by reference to tacit knowledge unsatisfactory.

23. I ignore here any representation of locations unoccupied by object surfaces.

24. Compare Pinker, "Mental Imagery and the Third Dimension."

25. In my view, scanning in two dimensions does typically proceed in this manner.

26. It is interesting to note that Kosslyn himself is sympathetic to the view that imagery involves symbol-filled arrays even though he does not endorse it. See Kosslyn et al., "Demystifying Imagery—Response to Commentators," p. 570.

27. I do *not* suppose either that the processes responsible for generating the various symbols in each cell are localized in the same place in the brain or that these processes are of the same sort. For a discussion of the location of the overall process of image generation, see chapter 8.

28. I am not claiming that cells representing adjacent patches really are adjacent in the brain, nor even that the arrays composed of such cells are physically localized.

29. For a defense of this view, see the writings of Jerry Fodor, for example, *The Language of Thought* (New York: Thomas Y. Crowell Company, 1975).

30. This point is well stressed by Jerry Fodor in "Imagistic Representation," in Block, *Imagery*, pp. 63–86.

31. See Hilary Putnam, "The Meaning of 'Meaning'," in *Minnesota Studies in the Philosophy of Science*, vol. 7, ed. by Keith Gunderson (Minneapolis: University of Minnesota Press, 1975).

32. Something, *x*, will be directly visible from viewpoint *V*, if, and only if, (a) *x* is visible from *V*, and (b) it is not the case that there is something, *y*, distinct from *x*, such that *x* is visible from *V* in virtue of *y*'s being visible from *V*.

33. See Pylyshyn " 'Mental Rotation' of Images."
34. By "smoothly" here I do not mean continuously (in the mathematical sense) but rather gradually.
35. See Shepard and Cooper, *Mental Images and Their Transformations.*
36. See Kosslyn, "Medium and Message," pp. 231–232.
37. See P. Carpenter and M. Just, "Cognitive Coordinate Systems: Accounts of Mental Rotation and Individual Differences in Spatial Ability," *Psychological Review* 92 (1985), pp. 137–172.
38. See Kosslyn, "Medium and Message," p. 232.
39. There is evidence that the rate does vary in one other way: as I mentioned earlier, back-to-front rotation is typically slower than rotation in two dimensions.
40. See Hinton, "Effects of Structural Descriptions in Mental Imagery"; also "Imagery without Arrays."
41. R. Finke and S. Pinker, "Emergent Two-Dimensional Patterns in Images Rotated in Depth," *Journal of Experimental Psychology: Human Perception and Performance* 6 (1980), pp. 244–264.
42. See S. Pinker, K. Stromswold, and L. Beck, "Visualizing Objects at Prespecified Orientations," paper presented at the annual meeting of the Psychonomic Society, San Antonio, November, 1984.
43. For ease of exposition, I ignore here the fact that some filled cells (those lacking what I earlier called "O-symbols") represent the color (and intensity) of locations unoccupied by any physical surface.
44. See Kosslyn, *Image and Mind* pp. 174–223; "Aspects of a Cognitive Neuroscience of Mental Imagery," *Science* 240 (1988), pp. 1621–1626; "Sequential Processes in Image Generation," *Cognitive Psychology,* forthcoming; and (with J. Roth) "Construction of the Third Dimension in Mental Imagery," *Cognitive Psychology* 20 (1988), pp. 344–361. I review the evidence cited by Kosslyn in chapter 6.
45. See also Farah et al., "Visual and Spatial Mental Imagery."
46. For more on connectionism, see D. Rumelhart, J. McClelland, and the PDP Research Group, *Parallel Distributed Processing,* 2 vols. (Cambridge, Mass.: MIT Press, 1986).

Chapter 6

1. See Berkeley, *Principles of Human Knowledge,* p. 10.
2. Dennett, "Nature of Images," in Block, *Imagery,* p. 55.
3. D. M. Armstrong, *A Materialist Theory of Mind* (London: Routledge and Kegan Paul, 1968), pp. 219–220.
4. Ultimately I want to deny that there are such properties. See chapter 7.
5. It might be objected that such properties as wearing shoes and wearing a belt are not visual. But it seems to me that they are, at least in the sense that they are visually detectable properties—one can tell by looking from an appropriate viewing position whether they are instantiated in a given case.
6. See Dennett, "Nature of Images."
7. Cases of impaired imagery in which subjects are unable to identify spatial relations among imaged objects do not directly threaten this claim, since such subjects may be unable to extract and cognitively process information that is implicitly contained in their images. An alternative hypothesis is that they are actually subject to two or more independent concurrent images, each representing its own object. For a discussion of this issue, see Tye, "Image Indeterminacy."

8. For ease of exposition I ignore here the fact that, on my view, some filled cells (those lacking what I earlier called "O-symbols") represent that certain locations unoccupied by any physical surface have a certain color (and intensity).

9. These relations will not automatically be identified by the imager, however, and in some cases (e.g., certain sorts of brain damage) it may not be possible for the imager to identify them. See here Tye, "Image Indeterminacy."

10. See Pylyshyn, "Imagery and Artificial Intelligence," pp. 174–176.

11. See Ned Block, "The Photographic Fallacy in the Debate about Mental Imagery," *Nous* 17 (1983), pp. 654–664.

12. See Pylyshyn, "Imagery and Artificial Intelligence."

13. See Block, "Photographic Fallacy."

14. I should stress that I am not, of course, mounting a general defense of the clear photographic view of percepts here.

15. The experiment described in the following sentences was performed by Neisser and Dirks and is reported by Ulrich Neisser in his "Tracing Mental Imagery," *Behavioral and Brain Sciences* 2, 4 (1979).

16. See Kosslyn, *Image and Mind;* Kosslyn et al., "Demystification of Mental Imagery"; and S. Kosslyn, "Sequential Processes in Image Generation," *Cognitive Psychology,* forthcoming.

16a. There is evidence that information about the visual appearances of objects and information about their spatial relations are stored separately in memory. See my discussion of "what" and "where" in Chapter 8.

16b. It seems plausible to suppose that for 4-year-old children the relevant comparison class of fluid levels here does not include those in the tilted feeding bottles they often saw when they were very young.

17. See Kosslyn, *Image and Mind.*

18. See Kosslyn, "Cognitive Neuroscience of Mental Imagery," p. 1622.

19. The effect of X mark position did not occur in a perception control task conducted by Kosslyn in which subjects were asked to decide whether the X mark actually did fall on a perceptually presented letter. See Kosslyn, "Cognitive Neuroscience of Mental Imagery."

20. See Pylyshyn, "Imagery and Artificial Intelligence."

20a. I want to stress that I am not claiming here that the children definitely do use visual images in the above experiment. My claim is rather that *if* they do, then there is no problem for the pictorialist. Of course, if they do not use images, then there is no problem either.

21. See Pylyshyn, "Imagery and Artificial Intelligence."

Chapter 7

1. Actually, I hold the broader view that there are no perceptual qualia, since I believe that the arguments I give below may be extended mutatis mutandis to the other senses. The outright rejection of qualia, both perceptual and nonperceptual, is defended by Daniel Dennett in his "Quining Qualia," in *Consciousness in Contemporary Science,* ed. by A. Marcel and E. Bisiach (Oxford: Oxford University Press, 1988); also by Gilbert Harman in "The Intrinsic Quality of Experience," in *Philosophical Perspectives* 4 (1990), ed. by James Tomberlin. I am sympathetic with some of the views expressed in these articles (and in several places I am indebted to Harman's discussion in particular), but I do not endorse their outright rejection of qualia. In particular, I think that nonrepresentational sensory states, for example, pain, do have qualia.

2. See Tye, "The Subjective Qualities of Experience," *Mind* 95 (1986), pp. 1–17; also Tye, *Metaphysics of Mind* chap. 6.

3. "By virtue of which" here does not mean *solely* by virtue of which. No one holds that the content of a visual experience is completely fixed by its qualia, just as no one holds that the content of a picture is completely fixed by the colors and shapes of its parts.

4. For a discussion of this issue, see chapter 8.

5. Here and throughout the chapter I use the term "visual experience" broadly to cover not only experiences brought about in normal sight but also hallucinatory and imagistic experiences.

6. This is to oversimplify a little. See my discussion of blind "sight" in section 7.2.5.

7. Compare Sydney Shoemaker, "Qualities and Qualia: What's in the Mind?", forthcoming.

8. See G. E. Moore, "The Refutation of Idealism," in *Philosophical Studies* (London: Routledge and Kegan Paul, 1922), p. 22.

9. This point parallels one made in chapter 1 for the case of mental images.

10. This view is taken by Gilbert Harman in "The Intrinsic Quality of Experience."

11. In something like the manner suggested by Kosslyn for mental images.

12. See Shoemaker, "Qualities and Qualia."

13. Assuming that the taste is indeed a chemical property of the wine. I am prepared to grant this assumption arguendo, but it is highly contentious.

14. See Shoemaker, "Qualities and Qualia."

15. In my view, this functional role can only be fully specified by a posteriori scientific investigation. I should add here that Shoemaker does quickly reject the view that what he likes is a combination of the content of the relevant experiences and their being produced by certain sense-organs. This view is similar to my proposal, but it is one that I too reject.

16. Just as hearing reveals to one nothing about the nature of sound, for example.

17. Shoemaker, in correspondence.

18. For more on alleged cases of qualia inversion, see section 7.2.6.

19. In fairness to Shoemaker, I should note that he does not himself view the example as decisive. See his comments in "Qualities and Qualia."

20. A case like that of Albert was suggested to me in conversation by Stephen Stich.

21. Since I am still using the term *visual experience* broadly to cover both the experience involved in seeing and imagistic experiences, I am not asserting here that *all* visual experiences play the same functional role in every respect. My claim is rather that there is a common functional core in virtue of which these experiences count as visual, notwithstanding their other functional differences. As in the earlier case of gustatory experience, a full specification of the relevant functional role will require reference to the findings of scientific psychology. Aspects of this role depend, I believe, on visual experiences' involving representations that have a special format (see chapter 5).

22. Knowing what it is like to see things requires that one undergo visual experiences. This is why Albert doesn't know what it is like to see.

23. Compare Sydney Shoemaker, "Functionalism and Qualia," *Philosophical Studies* 27 (1975), pp. 291–315; also Paul Churchland, *Matter and Consciousness* (Cambridge, Mass: MIT Press, 1988), pp. 39–40.

24. This is the line taken by Gilbert Harman in "The Intrinsic Quality of Experience." One problem that confronts such a line is that even if Tom's peculiarity is ultimately behaviorally detectable, it appears that some possible inversions are not, for example, inversions pertaining to the experiences of creatures who see the

world in black, white, and varying shades of grey. See Shoemaker, "Functionalism and Qualia."

25. This position, together with an internalist conception of knowledge that requires Tom to cite the belief that his experience represents a red object in any adequate justification of the claim that the tomato before him is red, entails that he does not know that the tomato is red. Indeed, more generally, it entails that he does not know the color of anything on the basis of vision despite his excellent performance. (I owe this point to Sydney Shoemaker.) Since the conclusion reached here is obviously false, I maintain that the above internalist conception of knowledge must be rejected.

26. Let me stress that the condition sketched here is *only* intended to be sufficient for Tom's experience to represent these things; it is *not* intended to be necessary. In general, I doubt that illuminating, naturalistic, necessary and sufficient conditions can be given for representational content. See chapter 8.

27. There are, I might add, any number of properties of this sort. Consider, for example, the property of being the loser.

28. In making these remarks as well as the earlier ones on population relativity, I am influenced by David Lewis. See his "Mad Pain and Martian Pain," in *Readings in Philosophy of Psychology*, ed. by Ned Block (Cambridge, Mass.: Harvard University Press, 1980), pp. 216–222. I do not endorse Lewis's combination of functionalism and type physicalism, however. For criticism of Lewis here, see M. Tye, "Functionalism and Type Physicalism," *Philosophical Studies* 44 (1983), pp. 161–174.

29. This view has it that *necessarily* any two brains undergoing exactly the same physical activity support exactly the same phenomenal states of consciousness. For more on supervenience, see chapter 8.

30. Assuming, of course, that the internal differences between cats and twin-cats are irrelevant.

31. See Christopher Peacocke, *Sense and Content* (Oxford: Oxford University Press, 1983). There is one difference between Peacocke's "sensational qualities" and perceptual qualia. According to Peacocke, sensational qualities are not qualities in virtue of which perceptual experiences have their contents. This difference, however, does not make a difference as far as my criticisms are concerned. (Peacocke does not say what the relationship is between sensational qualities and content. For some comments that are relevant to this issue, see note 32 and the surrounding discussion.)

32. One might try to rescue visual qualia here, or rather some close cousins, by holding that visual images and percepts have phenomenal qualities, conceived of as intrinsic, introspectively accessible properties that play no role as far as content is concerned (so that phenomenal qualities are *not* properties in virtue of which images and percepts have their contents). The problem now is that the view is not only counterintuitive but also even more mysterious: Why should there be such properties? What is their role?

Chapter 8

1. Property supervenience may be defined as follows: One property P supervenes on another property Q if, and only if, necessarily, for any time t and any object o, if o has Q at t, then o has P at t. The modal force of "necessarily" here is typically taken to be nomological in the strict sense (see section 8.3 for some comments on strict laws). In some discussions of supervenience, the temporal restriction is eliminated. In other discussions, further conditions are imposed. For the purposes of this chapter, I shall assume that property supervenience is as I

have just defined it. For more on the concept of supervenience in contemporary philosophy, see *The Southern Journal of Philosophy*, vol. 22, supplement containing the proceeding of the Spindel Conference on supervenience.

2. See L. G. Ungerleider and M. Mishkin, "Two Cortical Visual Systems," in *Analysis of Visual Behavior*, ed. by D. J. Ingle, M. A. Goodale, and R. J. W. Mansfield (Cambridge, Mass.: MIT Press, 1982), pp. 549–586.

3. See S. M. Kosslyn, "Seeing and Imagining in the Cerebral Hemispheres: A Computational Approach," *Psychological Review* 94 (1987), pp. 148–175.

3a. It is not easy to see how Kosslyn's position here can accommodate cases of impaired imagery in which patients can accurately image objects in previously witnessed scenes without being able to image their spatial relationships, unless the dorsal system is taken to contain two distinct subsystems, one concerned with the representation of locations of objects and the other with the representation of locations of parts of objects. For more on patients with the above impairment, see D. N. Levine, J. Warach, and M. J. Farah, "Two Visual Systems in Mental Imagery: Dissociation of 'What' and 'Where' in Imagery Disorders due to Bilateral Posterior Cerebral Lesions," *Neurology*, 35 (1985), pp. 1010–1018.

4. See M. J. Farah, M. S. Gazzaniga, J. D. Holtzman, and S. M. Kosslyn, "A Left Hemisphere Basis for Visual Mental Imagery?", *Neuropsychologia* 23 115 (1985), pp. 115–118; S. M. Kosslyn, J. D. Holtzman, M. J. Farah, and M. S. Gazzaniga, "A Computational Analysis of Mental Image Generation: Evidence from Functional Dissociations in Split-Brain Patients," *Journal of Experimental Psychology: General* 114 (1985), pp. 311–341; also Kosslyn, "Seeing and Imagining."

5. See Kosslyn et al., "Mental Image Generation."

6. I ignore here a series of control experiments that were also conducted to rule out various alternative accounts. See Kosslyn et al., "Mental Image Generation."

7. J. Deleval, J. De Mol, and J. Noterman, "La perte des images souvenirs," *Acta Neurologica Belgique* 83 (1983), pp. 61–79.

8. See M. J. Farah, "Neurological Basis of Mental Imagery."

9. See Kosslyn, "Cognitive Neuroscience of Mental Imagery."

10. The sum of the lawnmower's (actual) parts would not have been the same sum, if the spark plug had been changed.

11. Leibniz's law states that two items are numerically identical just in case every property possessed by either one of them is also possessed by the other.

12. Or alternatively the focus of one's attention remains fixed and what changes is the part of the pattern that falls under that focus, as the pattern is translated (during the scanning process) across the visual buffer. See section 3.3.

13. The fact that the firing pattern constituting M has P does not, of course, entail that M does not also have P. Although M and the firing pattern differ in some of their properties, P is not one of them.

14. Questions of the same general sort as this one have occupied a large number of philosophers. See, for example, Ted Honderich, "The Argument for Anomalous Monism," *Analysis* 42 (1982), pp. 59–64; Jaegwon Kim, "Epiphenomenal and Supervenient Causation," in *Midwest Studies in Philosophy* 9, ed. by P. French, T. Uehling, Jr., and H. Wettstein (Minneapolis: University of Minnesota Press, 1984); Ernest Sosa, "Mind-Body Interaction and Supervenient Causation," in French, Uehling and Wettstein, *Midwest Studies in Philosophy* 9; also Fred Dretske, *Explaining Behavior* (Cambridge, Mass.: MIT Press, 1988).

15. This point is nicely made by Brian McLaughlin in a recent defense of Davidson's anomalous monism against the charge that it makes mental properties epiphenomenal. See his "Type Epiphenomenalism, Type Dualism, and the Causal Priority of the Physical," in *Philosophical Perspectives* 3 (1989), ed. by James Tomberlin.

16. There is another possibility, namely, that M has P in virtue of having C. I ignore it in the text since it is obviously false.

17. I do not, of course, take this view with respect to every concept. One example of a concept that can be defined satisfactorily to my mind is the technical concept of a quasi-picture, as Kosslyn employs it.

18. This proposal is made by Jerry Fodor in "Making Mind Matter More," in his *A Theory of Content and Other Essays* (Cambridge, Mass.: MIT Press, 1990).

19. It might be objected that this is really better classified as a law of cognitive psychology, since experiments have been performed to support it (as noted in section 3.4). However, I am inclined to think that it is a law of both folk and cognitive psychology.

20. I owe this counterexample to Gabriel Segal.

21. A view of this sort is elaborated by Jaegwon Kim. See his "Epiphenomenal and Supervenient Causation."

22. (4), together with the revisions added below, is based on a proposal made by Gabriel Segal and Eliot Sober in their "The Causal Efficacy of Content," *Philosophical Studies*, forthcoming.

23. It must be remembered that the concept of supervenience employed in (4) is one that precludes property P from being instantiated at a different time from property P' (see note 1). This eliminates all putative counterexamples in which O had P before E occurs but after O had P' (as, for example, when O's having P' *causes* both E and O's having P).

24. One might try to defend (4) here by arguing that if F has inactive ingredients, it is false that your action, in virtue of being an application of F, causes the geraniums to grow dramatically. This seems very counterintuitive, however.

Index